Barney and Me

A. Roland Jay

To Sean
All the best!
Enjoy!

The photographs in this volume are from the collections of Wayne Cameron, Mary J. Gallant, Harley Ings, R. H. Inness, A. Roland Jay, Bill Rose and Wilfred Thompson.

Written by A. Roland Jay
© All rights reserved

ISBN 13: 978-1-928171-07-2 (pbk)
ISBN 13: 978-1-928171-08-9 (ebk)

Vocamus Community Publications
130 Dublin Street, North
Guelph, Ontario, Canada
N1H 4N4

www.vocamus.net

2014

I dedicate this book to the memory of my life-long friend, Donald "Barney" Ross, who passed away suddenly in Framingham, Massachusetts, on December 6th, 2013, his family by his side. At times, I could not have continued without his love, support and astute attention to detail.

Acknowledgements

Many thanks to my wife, Margaret Rose, who remained my constant mentor, computer technician, and sometimes editor throughout the writing of this book, and to all the others who gave freely of their encouragement and support. I could not have done it without you.

Preface

I started this memoir three years ago when I was relating to my thirteen year old grandson Eric and his two older brothers that I had been struck in the mouth with a hockey puck as a boy during a game of shinney on the outdoor rink in my home village of Mount Stewart, P.E.I. Eric innocently asked, "Where was your mouth guard?" I explained that I had only a used pair of skates with little or no ankle support, woolen mitts and a cheap boy's hockey stick.

That evening as I drove home I realized that I would be doing Eric and all other young hockey players in his generation a great injustice if I didn't record what it was really like trying to play hockey or any other sport in a small village on P.E.I. in the late 1940s and early 1950s.

This memoir is about some of the adventures that my friend Donald Ross and I had from roughly age six to sixteen, including conditions and facilities in our village during that time. I hope you enjoy it.

Barney and Me

A. Roland Jay

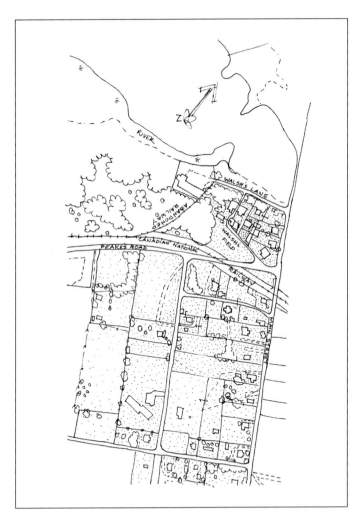

Map of South Side Mount Stewart

Chapter 1

Goodbye Fanningbrook,
Hello Mount Stewart

In October 1943, my family loaded our personal effects into the back seat of our 1933 Frontenac. My mother Marion and my three sisters, Eilleen, Connie and Muriel, climbed into the car and headed for our new home in Mount Stewart, roughly four miles away. That afternoon we had all helped pick, top and load the dump cart full with fresh turnips right from the field. When the ladies left, my father Roland and I followed, sitting on the front of the cart being pulled by my horse Dell, each of us on a side with our feet resting on a shaft, although I was practically standing, with our legs brushing against Dell's rump as she walked along. The shafts were short and strong, built for heavy loads, so the man usually sat with one foot ahead of the other. It was a beautiful early fall evening, and I remember the quiet solitude of that trip and how much of a 'little man' I felt, just being there alone with my father. I was still only five, due to turn six the next month, on November 2nd. From the Fan-

3

ningbrook road we turned onto the upper road to Mount Stewart. We were in the woods for a short time, then we passed a couple of clear fields to Bobby Ben's lane, then more woods before coming to Elmer Jay's open fields on the left, followed by his farmhouse and outbuildings. On the downhill on the right just past Elmer's was the People's Cemetery where my infant brother was laid to rest with most of my ancestors.

When we arrived at our new-to-us home in the village, my Mom and sisters were already there. I stayed with Dell while Daddy opened the outside hatch, so he could dump the load of turnips into the cellar. Dell didn't like to back up, and the ground near the hatch was inclined towards the house. When Daddy asked her to back up, she nearly put the cart through the side of the house. After Daddy got the cart into position he took out the tail gate, unhooked the latch at the front of the box, and physically dumped the turnips into the cellar. I helped round up the stray turnips that rolled away and threw them into the cellar. That load likely kept us and some of the relatives and neighbours in turnips for the winter.

During the move from the farm to the village, we took with us two milk cows, one yearling heifer, some laying hens and enough hay, oats and straw to feed and bed them. Daddy had cut a hole in the back wall of the cow stable for a manure hatch to throw out the manure from the animals. He also built a small door on hinges and a hook to keep the hole closed in winter. At the time, the practice of keeping animals in the village was freely accepted. Many of the neighbours did the same thing. After all, it was wartime and many necessities like tea, sugar, and molasses were rationed, and the more food you could generate yourself, the better. Rationing meant that each household was issued a book of coupons by the government and each purchase had to be accompanied by a coupon from the book. When the book was used up, then Mom or Daddy had to apply for another one. This practice continued until the War ended.

Just like the farmhouse we had left behind, our new home still had kerosene lamps and outdoor toilets. With no electricity and no running water, most homes had an outside pump and a bucket of water on a stand inside the house with a dipper beside it so anyone could have a drink. There was also another stand with a wash basin as well as the hot water tank on the end of the kitchen stove. In summer, we lowered our milk and butter in a bucket on a rope into an abandoned well in grandfather's back yard, to keep them cool. In winter, we simply kept them in the back porch or in the house at night.

All the bedrooms were upstairs, and under the beds were pots, some metal, some porcelain, to use for nature calls. These were dumped each day into a bucket, reserved for the purpose, called a slop pail, which was then carried by Mom or one of my two elder sisters to the outdoor toilet and dumped down the hole with the rest of the human deposits.

Aerial shot of Mount Stewart facing Northwest c.1940

Mount Stewart, c.1939

Chapter 2

After We Got Settled in the Village

Every fall, after we got settled in the village, my Mom's parents moved in from their home in the country and lived in the parlor of our house for the winter. Just imagine the supervision that was available to my sisters and me during the winter with one set of grandparents in our house and the other set across the driveway. If we were honest, we'd have to admit there was as much love as supervision. Mom's parents moved back to the farm each spring and repeated the procedure each winter until Mom's father passed away, when grandmother moved in to the other half of our house permanently.

Until this time, my friend Donald's grand uncle, 'Little Alex', his wife Ellie and his daughter Ramona, lived in the other half of our double tenement or duplex. At that time Alex and Ellie had no less than three sons overseas fighting in World War Two. After the war, Alex and Ellie moved out and went to live with their son Aeneas, who had returned home and built a new house just up the hill from our place.

Barney and Me

That was the first time my friend Donald and I had ever seen a cellar being dug. It was done by a man driving a horse pulling a scoop, which was really a giant spoon with a hook on the front that was hitched to the horse. It had two handles on the back for the driver to control and dump it. Like any other excavation, the man started by removing the sod and topsoil from the surface, the same as a bulldozer operator does today. He would set the scoop by raising the handles, command the horse to go ahead, and when the scoop was filled, he continued to the end and dumped it. Then he turned the horse around, reset the scoop, continued to the other end of the excavation and dumped it. In the early stages, he held a rein in each hand with the scoop handles, but as the horse got more accustomed to the task, the driver draped the reins around his neck and just touched them when he wanted the horse to change direction. He made many, many trips back and forth before the cellar reached the desired depth.

Me with my sisters, Eilleen, Connie and Muriel

Eilleen, Muriel, me and Connie

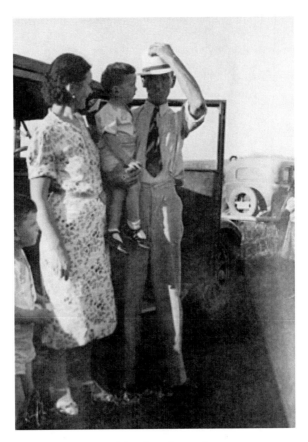

Mom and Dad with me in arms

Chapter 3

When I First Met Donald

I can't remember exactly when I first met my new neighbor Donald Ross, later nicknamed 'Barney', but it was soon after we arrived in the village. We became instant pals. He was ten months younger, having been born the September after me. We soon found out we had one big thing in common, that we were both the only boy in a family of sisters. I had three sisters, two older and one younger, and he had two, one older and one younger. We also had something different. I had my father home on weekends, and his father was overseas fighting the War. He lived next door with his Mom, Rita, and her Mom, Maggie Bell MacDonald, whom we all called 'Ma', at the telephone office, which they operated twenty-four hours a day, seven days a week. Another difference was that Donald's family was Roman Catholic and mine was Protestant, but we never let that come between us in spite of the attitudes of some adult members of both churches.

With few toys and no organized sports, we were left to our imaginations and devices to make toys like sling shots and bows and arrows, some of which didn't endear us to our sisters, parents or grandparents. It could be said that we were simply driven by a sense of wonder and adventure. As my grandfather Jay would say, "There's no tellin what mischief they'll get into." He and my grandmother, my father's parents, lived across his driveway from us on the opposite side from the telephone office. In a warning tone, Grammie's favourite reminder to Donald and me was, "You boys be good now, because Satan finds jobs for idle hands to do."

The front of Donald's house was very close to the sidewalk on Main Street, and the back yard ran back toward their barn, which was separated from our back yard only by a board fence. At the end of the barn next to the wagon trail was a large tree that we frequently climbed. We called it the 'dogberry' tree because of the red berries that came on it each year. We learned years later that it was really a Mountain Ash. To visit each other, we simply walked around the end of the board fence, and we were in the other's back yard.

Donald 'Barney' Ross and Me in a photo booth

Barney with his sisters, Jeanie and Adele

Barney with his grandmother, Ma, and his sister, Jeanie

Chapter 4

Bed Bugs and Other Pests

The first winter we lived in our new home in the village most of us children developed a rash on our chests that was quickly diagnosed as bed bugs. With mother's and grandmother's old fashioned remedies, we made it through the winter, and in the summer of '44 arrangements were made to have our place fumigated. This service is now known as tenting, and it involves sealing off all windows, doors and other openings, and then releasing cyanide pellets or similar poison inside the house. We had to vacate the place, and most of us went next door to Grampy Jay's. Others went to relatives or neighbours. Our eldest sister Eileen remembers that we were out of our house from Saturday morning until Sunday evening. Afterwards we moved back home, and life went on without the bed bugs, which never returned.

In those days, near the mirror above the kitchen sink, hung a small wicker basket that contained combs and brushes and a special fine-toothed comb. This comb was designed and used especially to remove head lice from

15

people's hair. Like the common cold, the flu and other viruses, head lice are easily distributed amongst children in schools. The effect of having lice was not as painful as bites from bed bugs, but the task of having them removed from our hair by the fine-toothed comb certainly was. The stigma attached to having them was more obvious, as well as the reflection on the personal hygiene of your family. In most homes of the day, without indoor plumbing, especially in winter, the shared water for Saturday night baths just didn't cut it, but it was the best our parents and most others could do.

With few concrete foundations and just root cellars under the houses, warm shelter and food was readily available to mice and rats, especially when the winds of winter approached. Mouse traps and rat traps were commonplace in most homes. Some of us boys learned early how to dispose of the latest catch from the night before, then bait and reset the mouse trap for the next victim. This was common if the man of the house was away working. During quiet times we would also play with an empty mouse trap by setting it and tripping it with a small stick, preferably in the presence of girls, to see if we could make them scream. Rat traps on the other hand were deemed by their large size and strength to be too lethal for young boys. We had to be big enough and strong enough before we were allowed to bait and set a rat trap.

Rats in the cellars of homes were common in winter,

around the old wharves by the river, and among the boulders along the river bank on both sides of the highway bridge in spring and summer. In the fall we could plan on rats migrating from the river to the barns and cellars of nearby homes. In no time, a single adult rat could mutilate the winter's supply of vegetables in the cellar. For this reason, most homes in the village had at least one adult house cat that had already proven its prowess as a hunter. It would make daily visits to the cellar in fall and winter to combat the invaders.

The best rat hunter we ever had was a tom cat called Stripesy, named for the stripes that ran over the top of his head between ears and down his neck. He considered hunting rats a sport, and in summer he patrolled the river bank almost daily, killing his prey, dragging it home, and leaving it lying on our front lawn for all to see. We would pet him and praise him, but before the day was out I would be invited to pick the rat up by the tail, carry it back down, and throw it on the river bank from whence it came.

My wife Margaret comes from Cape Breton Island, Nova Scotia where there are few skunks, but next door on Prince Edward Island we have our share of skunks and theirs too. Could it be because our island is smaller and more densely populated, with lots of old barns and buildings built close to the ground? Whatever the reason, from early childhood we learned that skunks were the enemy and must not be tolerated. It wasn't that the cute little furry kitten-like animal with the two white stripes down its back were so harmful. It was the smell!

Skunks are mostly nocturnal and the sighting of one scurrying across our backyard after dark caused an alarm to be sounded. This would bring our neighbour Angus running with loaded shotgun and flashlight. He cultivated a hate for skunks and took pleasure in emptying a load of buckshot into a skunk's rear end as it tried to dig its way under an old barn. He'd say,"Quick, grab the dog by the collar and hang on, so it doesn't get too close and get sprayed." If that happened, the dog would likely be banished from home and family for days, until the smell wore off. That was before the tomato juice shampoo was discovered.

Most of us have driven by a fresh carcass on the highway and scrambled to close the car windows, but the smell still gets in. Some of us have been less fortunate and driven over one with our vehicle. I have. We were on the way to a concert one evening. I just kept on going and wondered when we got there if anyone could smell us. If they did, they didn't mention it. I couldn't wait to get home and wash the car inside and out with the tomato juice shampoo.

Some people argue that skunks eat insects and rodents and are basically harmless, but oh, that smell. It's just too much!

Chapter 5

Lamps and Lanterns

Before the arrival of electricity, when daylight faded and darkness came, housewives and children relied heavily on lamps to complete their day's work. In the evening in our house, we gathered around the dining room table before dark to clean the lamp shades, refill the kerosene and trim the wicks if necessary. It was usually a family chore after supper and before lessons or homework. In winter when the days were shorter, it was done before supper. Most lamps had a reservoir for kerosene in the base which was accessible by removing a screw cap and inserting a small funnel. The adult, usually Mom, would say, "Fill to the top. Don't spill or overfill. Replace cap. Clean shades with clean, dry, soft cloth to remove smoke from previous use or wash in soap and water if needed." Most household lamps were glass or metal, with metal wick and shade holders, but some had a porcelain body with decorative paints, which would most likely be the parlour lamp. We didn't have one of those, just plain glass.

One evening while I was cleaning a lamp shade with a

piece of scrap winter underwear, I forced the rag into the bottom of the shade to clean a smoke stain from higher up inside the shade. Suddenly the shade around my hand snapped and a triangular piece popped out and fell on the floor. Luckily, the cloth was wrapped around my hand, and I didn't get cut. My Mom and sisters were startled, and Mom was upset because it meant the cost of a new shade, but she was happy I wasn't hurt. She considered a suspension from lamp cleaning as punishment, but that would free me from a daily chore, which would not please my sisters. Her conclusion was, "Just don't let it happen again!"

For those homes that could afford it, or that had inherited one, the Aladdin lamp was the Cadillac of lamps. It was powered by a refined liquid gas called naptha, and as part of the filler cap, it had a plunger with a hole in it that pushed air down into the reservoir. This created pressure to drive vaporized gas up into the mantle, which was a fire proof dome-shaped mesh that gave off a light far superior to a kerosene lamp. The shade on the Aladdin was a tall, thin glass tower that magnified the light from the mantle. Mantles were very fragile, especially when hot, and expensive to replace, but would last for a long time if handled with care.

The lantern, on the other hand, was even more basic than the kerosene lamp and more rugged. In addition to the tank at the bottom, it had a u-shaped frame that supported the entire upper structure including a smoke stack on top. The lantern also had a long, wire carrying handle that was fastened to both sides of the frame near the top. Unlike the lamp, the glass shade in the lantern was in the middle surrounded by a wire cage to protect it from breakage if the lantern fell or got knocked over.

One evening after dark, our first winter in the village, I carried a lit lantern for my eldest sister Eileen when she and I went to the barn to milk the cow. I left the lantern sitting on the floor behind the cow so my sister could see what she was doing. Part way through the milking something spooked the cow, and she jumped, knocking over the lantern. The light went out, and the cow ended up with a hind foot in the part bucket of milk. We were left in the dark but were thankful the light went out. It could have easily set the barn on fire, and we would have been in real trouble. That was the end of the milk. Mom was angry at the both of us, but happy we didn't burn the barn down.

Daddy used a more compact, tougher version of the barn lantern when he worked on the railroad. It was equipped with either a clear or red shade, depending on the task he had. That kerosene lantern was later replaced by a battery operated one with two bulbs that was more reliable and less messy to work with.

A fox in a fox ranch

A water dish and a scraper used for cleaning fox hides

Chapter 6

Grampy Jay's Fox Ranch

In 1943, when we first moved from the farm into the village and Daddy was away working on the railroad, his father became my temporary father figure. One of the major attractions to me was Grampy's fox ranch, just down past the old wharf by the river. Mornings and evenings whenever I could, I went with Grampy to feed the foxes. We would first go to his barn and fill a galvanized bucket with dry cubes of fox feed from a barrel that was tightly covered to keep the rats out. Then we would walk past his house, down his driveway to the river, and follow a well worn path past Walsh's house, over a little brook to the ranch. Grampy walked ahead, and I tagged along.

The ranch was an assortment of fox pens inside a high board fence with only one door through it. The door was cut off above the ground so I had to step high over the bottom portion of the fence to get inside. That was because the bottom of the whole fence around the ranch had chicken wire stapled to it with the leading

23

edge buried in the ground. This was to prevent a fox from digging its way out under the fence should it escape from its pen. Before entering the ranch, Grampy warned me to stay clear of the pens and above all, he warned, "Don't stick your fingers through the wire mesh, or the fox will bite them off."

The ranch had twenty-five or thirty pens in rows. Each was made of a wooden frame with a pitched board roof and a small door on one end that would allow him to reach inside to feed and water the foxes. Most of the outside skin of each pen was wire mesh except for one corner at the back that was boarded in for shelter. In that corner was also a fox house or den, a small cube-shaped wooden box with a round hole in front big enough to let the foxes in or out. The den also provided additional shelter from the weather. The floors of the pens were wooden boards nailed tightly together to deter attempts at escape. Foxes are sly, timid and easily spooked. Sometimes as we approached a pen and a fox was sitting on top of his den, it would jump down and scurry inside.

Each pen would hold a pair of adult foxes and their family if it was the right time of year. On the other hand, there might only be one fox in some pens if it was necessary to isolate it from the others, because it was a breeding male, or sick, or just plain anti-social. Most of the foxes were of the silver variety, dark in color with silver hair mixed in and a white tip on their tail.

Grampy, who was a rather large man, huge in my

little eyes, would visit each pen, open the door, reach in for the feed dish and dump it out. Then he would fill it with fresh food. He would do the same to the water dish. The dishes were all the same, enamel coated metal, beige in color with a red band around the top, about eight inches in diameter and two inches deep. Each dish had a small hole drilled through the rim and was attached to the wire mesh near the door by a short strand of straight wire. This was to prevent the foxes from dragging it to the back of the pen where Grampy couldn't reach it. During our visits, the foxes would usually stay in their dens and watch us.

The ranch was open to the sky, and during a severe winter storm the snow banks might drift high enough to cover the top of the outside fence. If a fox managed to escape from its pen, it could easily run up the snow drift, out over the fence, and be gone. When Grampy discovered this during one morning feeding, he checked for tracks in the snow to get some idea which way the fox had gone. He sounded the alarm with other ranchers to form a search party to find the fox.

At a time like this, Grampy would also call his friend, Chester Birt from Pisquid East, and if he was available, Chester would bring his big, mostly Great Dane hound dog to track the missing fox. Why all the fuss? Well, in those days, fox fur for the ladies was big business. These animals were very valuable, especially in winter when their fur was prime, and even more so if the escapee was a purebred adult. The men would examine the fox tracks in the snow and agree on the most likely direction the fox had gone, often to a clump of woods within sight of the ranch. If the river was still frozen, the tracks might lead across the ice to the other side. The search party would set out on foot, on snowshoes, on horseback or on horse and sleigh, with Chester and his dog in the lead. I was too small to go, so I didn't know much about what happened until they returned with or without the fox. It might be late in the day or even after dark by the time they got back. If they were unsuccessful, they might go again the next day. They told me when they found the fox, they surrounded or cornered it and captured it. If the dog got there first, he would run the fox down, pounce on it and hold it until Chester or someone else got there.

Late every winter, when the fox fur was prime, came skinning time. In addition to killing and skinning his own select foxes for that year, Grampy had his workshop set up with three skinning stations for custom work, manned by two hired skinners and himself. Each station had a short rod hanging from the ceiling with hooks on both sides to hang the foxes by the hind legs for skinning. The foxes would arrive, usually at night, in trunks, in back seats of cars, or in pick-up trucks. If Donald and I were there, we'd help carry the dead foxes into Grampy's barn and place them carefully in rows on the floor. Some of the bodies would still be warm. Under no circumstances were we to pile one body on top of another, or let them even touch each other. That was because the heat from their bodies would cause a part in the fur that could not later be corrected. Grampy's barn was wired with electric lights so the men could work at night. That was a really big deal in those days, but most of the skinning was done during the day. It was an assembly line of sorts, where young boys like Donald and me would come in handy as runners on evenings and Saturdays.

Usually Grampy and the two helpers would be busy skinning, and when they needed more foxes from the barn, Donald and I would fetch them. We would also carry the fox pelts now mounted on boards into Grampy's kitchen where Grammie and two other ladies were finishing the process. In a corner, just inside the workshop door, was a small pot-belly stove that burned scraps of wood, mostly to keep the place warm. If the fire burned down, one of the men would throw a handful of fox fat on it to get going again. Phew! What a stink that made coming out the stove pipe into the cold winter air.

When the men started to skin a fox, they'd slit the hind legs with a sharp knife, just above the heel, and hang the fox upside down on the two hooks hanging from the ceiling. First, they would slit between the hind legs toward the belly, then slit in the opposite direction along the underside of the tail far enough to reach in and grab the tail bone. They then grasped the outside of the tail with their other hand and pulled the bone right out of the tail. Later they split the tail all the way to the end.

Next they skinned the hind legs by separating the bone from the skin down to the toes. There they used side cutters to snip the little bones of the toes so the paw would remain intact. They'd later do the same to the front legs. As in skinning any animal, they cut along the inside of the pelt to separate it from the body taking care not to cut the hide. At the same time they kept a downward pull with their other hand until they reached the head. Here they cut even more carefully around the ears and eyes, leaving the ears with the pelt and the eyes with the body. The finished head would later be fitted with glass eyes. Then they continued down to the snout, which they cut off the body so it remained with the pelt, now completely inside out.

The pelt was then stretched, tail first, over a smooth board with a tapered end at the top to fit the head. The body was tossed outside the workshop on a pile of bodies at the base of a tree, which would later be picked up by a farmer with a horse and sleigh from down river. We were told he fed them to the pigs.

The pelt now showed hide and some fat to the outside, fur inside, four legs and tail dangling from the board. It was stood up on end and lined up with others against the back wall of the workshop. When Donald and I showed up, it was our job to carry these greasy fox pelts on boards to Grampy's kitchen where Grammie and two neighbor ladies finished tacking the pelts to the boards with shoe tacks for drying. The hind legs were attached to the outside edge of the board and the front legs were tacked to small, tapered pieces of wooden shingles specifically for the purpose. The ladies then scraped the remaining fat off the inside of the pelts using small blocks of hardwood, designed and crafted by Grampy, sharpened on one edge and made to fit a woman's hand.

When finished, the boards with fox pelts would be lined down both sides of the front hall where the heat from the furnace would help the drying. On the kitchen floor, Grammie had saucers filled with water to catch the fleas that left their cozy place in the fox fur. When drying was complete, each pelt was removed from its board, turned right side out, brushed, cleaned and bundled to be sent to the furrier in the city. It might be shipped all over the northern hemisphere for fashionable ladies to wear around their shoulders on cold winter nights.

Within five years from that time, however, the market for fox fur dried up, and Grampy with all the other ranchers got out of the business. It was said that some of the ranchers just opened the doors of their pens and let their foxes run loose. Evidence of that is still visible today in wild red foxes on P.E.I. that have hints of silver in their coat, and some even have white tips on their tails.

Chapter 7

Uncle Reaney

As mentioned earlier, I was born in a farmhouse in a rural community called Fanningbrook on P.E.I. That farm was where my father and his sister were born and raised, and Daddy still farmed it at that time. My father's father and twelve siblings, eight brothers and four sisters, were also born and raised in that same community. We came from a long line of fiercely religious people of the protestant faith in the Methodist Church who, it was said, totally abstained from everything but hard work, good food, music, fun, laughter and raising large families.

The second youngest of my grandfather's family was a boy named Reaney who lived and farmed across the brook from our place. Reaney had a reputation of not toeing the line and being a little rough around the edges. Unlike most of his relatives, who were total abstainers, Reaney was known to take a wee dram occasionally. He was not particular about his behaviour, about how he dressed or about what people thought of him.

Barney and Me

Reaney had a dog named Toby, and every morning or evening you could hear Reaney trying to control the unleashed, disobedient dog by shouting at him over and over again, "Toby here," while walking to his back fields to retrieve his cows for milking. Daddy used to mimic him calling the dog, just for laughs, in a good natured way.

Later I grew up and joined the R.C.M.P., and when I came home on leave, stories of Reaney's exploits still prevailed. After several years working in uniform in rural Cape Breton, Nova Scotia with the police force, I was transferred to a three man plain clothes unit in Sydney. There we specialized in enforcement of Federal Statutes like Customs and Excise Acts, which prohibit smuggling and making illicit spirits (moonshine). We received a monthly bulletin that included a list of recent seizures of stills and illicit spirits in eastern Canada. At the time my boss was a rather gregarious, boisterous character. One morning, while all three of us were in the office, he was reading the latest copy of the bulletin and abruptly in a loud voice said, "Hey Jay, what's this?" He then proceeded to read aloud an item where Uncle Reaney and his son had been caught making moonshine from a still in their farmhouse in Fanningbrook, P.E.I. Talk about life's embarrassing moments! For several weeks thereafter, the same boss, and others who heard about it, took great pleasure reminding me about my law-abiding relatives back home.

Chapter 8

Stuttering

When I was a small boy, I had learned to talk in the usual way. I was an excitable red head with a bad temper. At the age of seven, after almost continuous consecutive communicable diseases (e.g., measles, chicken pocks, and whooping cough), our doctor decided to send two of my sisters and me to the hospital in the city to have our tonsils removed. In the process, the surgeon cut my tongue-tie. At age seven, it was my first trip to the hospital and, in spite of my mother and two sisters being there, I was scared.

It was my first and only operation. I remember being given ether for the anesthetic and drifting off to sleep. When I awoke back in the ward, I cried for my Mom and raised such a ruckus that the nurses had to move me to a private room. There they gave me ice water to sooth my throat and help calm me down. That was the first time I had ever seen machine-made ice cubes.

When I recovered and was sent home, it wasn't long before I began to stutter. It was always worse when I got excited, especially in adult company and thought I had something to add to the conversation. It was even worse when my sisters or school mates would tease me, though Donald never did, always supporting me in my predicament.

My parents were very concerned about this development and somewhat embarrassed, especially in mixed company. When we went visiting, Daddy's strategy was to sit beside me with his legs crossed. If I started to stutter, he would tap me on the shin with his free foot to get my attention and slow me down or stop me altogether. There were no speech therapists in those days, or if there were, they were in the city and we didn't know of them. But with tender love and guidance from my parents, grandparents and concerned neighbours, I gradually overcame this curse, and rarely does it visit me today. I also found, as did my family, that singing seemed to relax and stabilize me in stressful situations.

There's a cute little story that my friend Jim Youden from Newfoundland used to tell about a deckhand who stuttered. His captain had heard him sing earlier in the voyage and marveled at his beautiful voice. A few days later in a wicked storm at sea, the deckhand was going from the bow to the stern when the cook opened the galley door and was swept overboard. The deckhand ran up to the wheelhouse and tried to tell the Captain what had happened, but all he could say was "Ca-, Ca-, Ca-, Ca-, Ca-, Ca." After several minutes of this, the frustrated Captain said, "For God's sake man, if you can't say it, sing it." The deckhand sang in slow melodious tones: "Should old acquaintance be forgot, and never brought to mind, the bloomin' cook fell overboard, he's forty miles behind."

Chapter 9

Pigeon Toes

At the same time in my life as I was combating stuttering, I was also walking pigeon-toed, with my toes turned inward and on the outside edge of my feet. If I was in a hurry I leaned forward, and it was difficult to keep my balance. This too was a source of torment from friends and schoolmates alike, Donald excepted.

Our doctor or someone else suggested lying on my back in bed, doing exercises by forcing my toes to the outside and holding them there as long as I could or until it hurt. I did this religiously every night before I went to sleep, and later I tightened the top sheet so I could lock my feet in that position while I slept. It took at least a year of conscious effort both standing and walking before I could automatically walk with my feet pointed straight ahead. One effect of this early condition could be seen on the outside of the heels of my well-worn shoes or boots, because that part of the heel was more worn than the rest. But, I'm still walking, and very thankful for it.

Chapter 10

The Telegram

I mentioned previously that Donald's father was overseas fighting World War Two. Before I met Donald, during the summer of 1943, his father had been home on a short leave to visit with his family, which was thoroughly enjoyed and fondly remembered by all. One morning in May of 1944, the CNR station agent, Harry MacKay, called the telephone office and asked Donald's mother to send her uncle, Little Alex, over to the station for a message. Donald and I were out playing in his backyard. A short time later we were startled by the sounds of people crying in the house. Soon his older sister burst from the back door, sobbing, and told us that their father had been killed overseas. We stopped what we were doing for a short while, agreed that big boys don't cry, and carried on playing. Later, Donald's Mom came to the back door and called him into the house, and I went home.

For the longest time, Donald and I never spoke of that sad day. Donald's father, Pte. Alexander Joseph Ross Reg. #F59996, was a member of a Maritime Regiment that, over a period of four years, had marched from the Southern tip of Italy to within a few miles of the border of France. It was near the end of that march, while they were camped one morning, that enemy planes bombed the camp, and Sandy was struck by shrapnel and died on May 23, 1944. He was buried in a military cemetery at Casino, Italy. This event seemed to bring Donald and I even closer together and more like the brothers that we never had.

This is a little story related to Donald by his Mom, Rita, when he was older, about his father and his early smoking habits: When his father was home on leave from the War in 1943, Donald was only five years old. Someone had left a cigarette burning in an ash tray, Donald spied it and decided to have a few puffs. It wasn't long before he was caught, scolded and told never to do that again. A few days later, he crawled up onto his father's lap while his father was smoking a pipe. Dad decided to teach the son a lesson and offered him a puff of the pipe. The joke was on Dad because Donald took a puff, didn't cough or choke, and enjoyed it so much that Dad had to take the pipe away from him.

Chapter 11

Then There Were Three

In the years following the end of World War Two, it was
normal to see airmen, soldiers and sailors return home
to the village and surrounding communities. Some of
them Donald and I could barely remember, and some we
had never seen before. None of this was easy on Donald
because it only reminded him that his own father was
never coming back.

One of the returned men, Freeman Affleck, brought
back a war bride, and they moved in next door to the
Telephone Office (Donald's house) and lived on the second floor of Alden and Jean's house. They had an infant
son who, when he became old enough, received a new
red scooter from his grandparents overseas, the likes of
which Donald and I had never seen. It even had white
wall balloon tires. All Donald and I had were beat up
used bicycles with chains that were always falling off. Oh
how we wanted to try out that scooter, but our parents
told us to keep our hands off. Freeman got a job with
the Deptartment of Highways driving a bulldozer in sum-

mer that became a snowplow in winter with a 'V' plow attached.

The sons of our next-door neighbours, Ellie and Little Alex returned as well – Anaeas, Francis and Vernon. They and many more that we didn't know so well also returned. What a joyous time! Without exception, all of these heroes made a fuss over Donald and me, the brats of the block. They seemed always to have time to stop and talk to us and tease us about girls or comment on some recent happening.

Around 1946, a family from Porter's Lake, Nova Scotia moved into the village on our side of the bridge. I think the father of the family was a returned Air Force veteran, but I'm not sure. He and his wife had one son named Allan who was our age and went to our school. He seemed nice enough but didn't know anyone, so Donald and I made friends with him, tried to show him around, and included him in some of our adventures. Allan's father Robie was the new Rawleigh man for the village and surrounding area, so he travelled door to door or farm to farm pedaling his wares. Some of you near seniors may recall Rawleigh and Watkins products such as medicated ointment, a cure-all for any malady, assorted lineaments, spices and other handy remedies for the home, and fly spray to keep the flies off the milk cows during milking.

Robie didn't have a car, so his sole means of transportation was horse and wagon in summer and horse and sleigh in winter. To Donald and I this meant another rig that we could hitch a ride on, especially when Mr. Bond would be coming home in the evening. All three of us might help to unhitch the horse and put him away in the barn for the night.

In those days, there was a silly song on the radio called "Barney Google", and the chorus went like this – "Barney Google with the goo-goo-googly eyes." Allan saw some similarity between the song and his new friend Donald. Over a period of time, in a most friendly way, Allan nicknamed Donald 'Barney', and it stuck. I rarely used it, because I had enough with nicknames, having at least half a dozen of my own associated with my red hair, but some friends call him that to this day. The Bonds stayed in the village only a couple of years and then moved back to Nova Scotia.

Chapter 12

Amos in the Outhouse

In our part of the village in the early 1940s, there was no indoor plumbing, so every house had an outdoor toilet somewhere on the property. About that time Grampy Jay tore out an old orchard and built a new house to rent on the lot between the river and what would later become our house. He also built a toilet in the back yard right against the board fence that separated that yard from our future back yard.

Before we moved in, and for a little while after, Donald's grand uncle, Little Alex, and his wife Ellie lived in the other half of our house. Little Alex had a green '41 Ford half ton known as 'The Green Hornet' because it could really scat with its owner at the wheel. He usually came home for dinner at Noon and parked the truck unlocked, with the keys in it, like most everyone did in those days. It was always parked in the driveway beside his place facing down a slight grade towards the board fence that separated his back yard from the neighbours'.

One day around Noon in the summer of '43, when

Donald was not yet five years old, he was at Little Alex's sitting on the front seat of the truck playing car. Like all boys his age, he would sit and turn the steering wheel back and forth (no power steering), make motor noises with his mouth, and pretend to be shifting gears. On this day, Donald accidentally put the truck out of gear, and it started to roll forward down the grade toward the fence, gaining speed as it went. Donald's legs were too short to reach the brake pedal. The truck crashed into the fence, knocking out a section into the back of neighbour Amos' outhouse. The impact tipped the outhouse over onto its front door, with Amos in it! Donald jumped out of the truck and 'took to his scrapers' down the hill to home. When Alex and Ellie came out to see what the racket was, they saw the truck in the fence, the bottom of the outhouse pointing towards them, with Amos on his hands and knees inside, looking out through the hole hollering, "Get me outta here!"

Chapter 13

The Telephone

Shortly after we moved into the village, our new telephone was installed just inside the kitchen door on the dining room wall. It was a large wooden box with an adjustable mouthpiece on the front center and a receiver with a cord that hung on a hook on the left hand side. When the receiver was on the hook, the line was disconnected. When it was removed, the line was open, and we could use the crank on the right hand side to ring 'central' or someone on our party line. Two bells were mounted on the top front of the box with a striker between them, so when another party called our house or any other house on our party line, the bells would ring loudly. On the bottom front of the box was a slanted shelf if we needed to write something down. A private line was available, but it cost more, so most homes were on a party line. Our number was two long rings and one short.

Party lines were the source of much irritation to fellow subscribers, mostly when someone would hear the other's ring on the line and pick up to listen in on the conversation. Many stories abound about this practice, both good and bad, some funny and some not so funny. This is one such story:

Before stove and furnace oil, most stoves in the village burned wood, coal or both. Much of the wood came from farmers in the country who owned woodlots and had surplus firewood for sale. Such a farmer was a middle aged bachelor named Cy Driscoll. One of his favourite customers in the village was Vi Corrigan, a spinster about his age, whose winter wood supply was exhausted by the time the frost started to come out of the ground in the spring. When this happened, rural dirt roads became almost impassable, especially in low-lying sections. After church on Sunday, Vi spoke to Cy about getting a load of firewood from him sometime soon. They each were on a different party line.

Monday and Tuesday of the next week the weather was mild, and it seemed that the bottom just dropped out of the roads. They were unfit to travel. However, the forecast for Wednesday night was a heavy frost that would freeze the road surface hard enough to carry a load of firewood from Cy's to Vi's. Wednesday evening Vi called Cy to remind him that tomorrow morning might be a good time to deliver her wood. When the phone rang at Cy's that evening, the eavesdroppers on his line picked up. They listened intently, each hoping to hear something spicy between Vi and Cy. The conversation

44

was cordial but short. Cy's innocent closing remark was said to be, "Okay then, Vi. If it stiffens up tonight, I'll run it into you in the marnin."

The eavesdroppers could barely get their phones hung up before bursting into uncontrollable laughter. That story has been repeated many times throughout the community ever since, much to the joy of those who never heard it before.

Rural telephone lines were part of a cooperative system, where poles were cut, hauled out of the woods and erected along the road and across the fields. Likewise, wires were acquired, installed and maintained by subscribers, the men of the community. If a storm knocked down poles or wires, the men went out the next day, sometimes in waist deep snow, found the damage and temporarily repaired it, even running telephone wires along the fences. Later when spring came, they would repair the poles and lines completely.

Luther going fishing in the river

Fishing smelt through the ice with bag nets

Chapter 14

The River

The Hillsboro River flows through Mount Stewart and more or less splits it in two. One of the headwaters of the river is Fanningbrook, the brook that gave the name to where I was born and the community where our original ancestors settled. My grandfather Jay and his twelve siblings were all born and raised there, as well as my father and his sister.

My three sisters and I were born in a relatively new farmhouse built by my father and grandfather on the same site as the old farmhouse, then a granary. We were all delivered with the assistance of a midwife, and the doctor from the village attended as soon as he could afterwards, to check mom and baby and cut the umbilical cord, if that had not already been done. As for conveniences, the house had a kitchen sink with gravity-fed cold water from a tank in the loft above the kitchen. We also had a wood burning kitchen stove with a copper hot water tank on one end. The water was pumped by a small gasoline engine attached to a converted manual pump in the pump house, up through a small steel pipe into a large tank above the kitchen. A similar pipe carried the cold water down to the lone tap in the sink, which drained out into the field behind the house.

At the end of our lane next to the road was a small pool where the source of the brook bubbled up out of the ground. Between there and the lane was a space where horses could be driven into the brook to stop and drink while still attached to whatever conveyance they were pulling. Passersby and neighbors were also welcome to use this location for the same purpose.

Although Hillsboro was always referred to as The River, it's really an estuary. The tide rises and falls up to within a mile of the head. Mount Stewart is about two miles south of the head. From the village to where it dumps into the Charlottetown harbor twenty some miles away, it has many stories to tell, including Donald's and mine. In winter, in spite of some salt content, the river freezes over completely except for the fast moving water between the wharves and under the bridges. These were danger spots and parents always warned us to steer clear of them. The wharves faced each other and were about forty feet apart, two hundred yards downstream from the highway bridge. Only once did I skate across the river between the wharves and the bridge when it was frozen enough to carry me. I was going to play hockey at the rink, put my skates on at home and took a short cut. When my Mom found out, I never did it again.

Barney and Me

In the winter, a life-long fisherman named Luther lived in the village and fished smelt between the two wharves. He used a bag net strung between two long poles, weighted and stuck in the mud in the bottom of the river. He would set the net on the incoming tide and haul it in before the tide turned. Luther and his wife Flossie had no children, so he would invite Donald and me to go with him on Saturdays or at night to help haul the nets. Unlike today, hauling the traps was all done by hand, and you had to be strong to do it. We weren't very strong, but we were agile and quite at home on the water.

Luther fished from a flat-bottomed boat that was three feet wide and maybe ten feet long that he called a punt. The punt was sturdy and unlikely to upset. At night we operated by the light of a Coleman gas lantern. There we learned that our homemade woolen mitts were warmer when wet with a coating of ice on the outside. Our reward for helping Luther was a feed of smelt or a trout that had followed the smelt into the net looking for a snack of spawn. Whatever it was, we would gladly take it home to our mothers. At the time, we didn't re-alize it, but our greatest reward was what Luther taught us about the river, the changing tides and the different species of fish that survived the winter under the ice.

In the spring, Luther also fished lobsters out of Savage Harbour on the North shore, six miles from the village. Donald wasn't with me the spring that I was fourteen when I worked in the lobster cannery at Savage Harbour for a short time. One day the owner of the cannery came and announced that because of the high demand for live lobsters on the eastern seaboard of the U.S., he was forced to shut the cannery down. That same day one of Luther's helpers was sick, and Luther invited me to go fishing lobsters in his place the next day. I went with him one day, but the next day his helper was better and came back to work, so I moved on.

Chapter 15

'Smokin'

Until the red flags went up in the 1960s and 1970s, warning us of just how harmful tobacco products were to our lungs, heart and mouth, smokin, chewin, and spittin were the most macho things a man, or even a boy, could do. I started smoking when I was about eight, and Donald was right beside me at age seven. Early on, Donald had more opportunity for butts from ash trays, because there were smokers in his house. Nobody smoked in our house, until Daddy took up the habit after I left home. Donald also had roll-your-own tobacco and papers available, which were easy to pinch a bit at a time and difficult for adults to detect. Later, in Donald's house and others, they had a table top manual machine that allowed the user to make custom roll-your-owns that looked almost as good as tailor made. There was no shortage of ignition sources, due to easy access to a large box of wooden matches on the stove top or wall above every kitchen stove.

One of Donald's and my early adventures with cigarettes involved his grand uncle Little Alex's pick-up truck, parked in the driveway next to his house at noon. Little Alex's daughter Ramona looked out her kitchen window and saw the two of us coming away from the truck, which everyone called The Green Hornet, heading for my father's barn. She followed and found us sitting one on each side of the pitch hole to the hayloft before we had time to light the two cigarettes that we had taken from her father's truck. Ramona chewed us out royally, ordered us down from the loft, took the cigarettes from us and went back to the house. We're not sure if she ever told anybody about this. Maybe she didn't want to mention it. She was a teenager who also smoked, so maybe she kept the cigarettes for herself. As for Donald and me, we never tried that trick again.

When house and car sources ran dry, there were always the streets and roads where we could gather butts on dry days. If we found one that had been stomped on, we'd rescue the tobacco from it and stash it until we could acquire a paper or two and attempt to roll our own. The early models were kind of shabby, but we got better with practice. The best find was a butt that had been thrown from a vehicle and gone out. One sunny day I found a butt on the roadside that had barely been smoked. When we read the label, we knew right away why it had been discarded, and laughed about it. That particular brand tasted awful! I kept it anyway, in an abandoned oat box in our horse barn, and named it 'my big Buckingham'.

We later expanded our habit and started smoking pipes. Donald splurged and bought a corn cob pipe at Woolworth's 5 and 10 cent store in the city. It was hot on the tongue and was short lived. Earlier we had tried carving out the center of horse chestnuts with our pocket knives, and we attached dried golden rod stalks to them as pipe stems. We used old tobacco, but the experiment failed because we were unable to get the stem to fit tightly enough to the chestnut. If we managed to get it lit, the end of the stem in the bowl caught fire and also burned our tongues.

We had several secluded places outdoors where we could light up, have a puff and manage, we thought, to go undetected. When we made some money, we'd split the cost of a package of tobacco and papers, hide it in the barn or woodshed, and make it last as long as we could. When we got older, Donald and I would also chip in with friends to buy a package of tailor made cigarettes when we travelled together as big shots in trucks or went to dances. By then we were facing the challenge of inhaling a full drag of smoke and feeling the nausea that went with it, but we prevailed, and managed to get hooked.

As we got older our addiction forced some difficult decisions. On P.E.I., classes in the rural schools only went as high as Grade Ten, so to attend senior high we had to go to college in the city. Most of us boarded in private homes from Sunday to Friday evening. On Sunday nights when Daddy dropped me off at the boarding house, he'd give me five dollars for the week's room and board and five cents as spending money. Most weeks I'd carry the nickel in my pocket until Wednesday trying to decide if I would buy two cigarettes illegally at the corner store or get a chocolate bar. I usually bought the cigarettes. I also had an ace in the hole in my eldest sister Eileen, a graduate R.N., who worked nearby at the Polyclinic. Some weeks she'd take pity on me and give me a dime or even a quarter if she felt flush.

After many failed attempts at quitting as an adult, I finally quit at age forty-three.

Chapter 16

Uncle Wilfred

From the time we moved into the village, every chance he got, Uncle Wilfred kept pestering Daddy about buying my horse Dell. Each time, if I was near, I was all ears and ready to object. Wilfred used all the rationale he could think of: Daddy was away all the time working on the railroad, and Dell was doing nothing but standing in her stall, eating and needing someone to clean up behind her. There was no field to turn her out in, and Wilfred had a whole farm for her to work and play on, and none of the current situation was doing the mare or Daddy any good. His final plea was in our kitchen one evening when he told Daddy that he really needed Dell to replace one of his older horses that was getting too old to do hard work. Daddy knew Wilfred would give Dell a good home and not abuse her, so he accepted $144.00, which seemed to me like a ton of money, but in my eyes she was worth every cent. Too late I realized the deal was done, and I kicked up such a fuss that Wilfred leaned over, gently picked me up and sat me on his knee. He promised me that any evening, any weekend, any school vacation, all I had to do was call, and he would come to the village and take me over to his place to visit Dell, even stay overnight. Wilfred was the third of Mom's five older brothers and one of her favourites.

So began my many wonderful trips to Uncle Wilfred's at Savage Harbour to see Dell. The first time I stayed overnight, I slept with Uncle Wilfred because he was alone in a double bed. One morning at breakfast, after I had been driving Dell and Jack the previous day, Wilfred teasingly related to the whole family how in the middle of the night he was abruptly awakened by me sitting up in bed, apparently asleep, "hollerin and shoutin and still driving horses." Everyone got a good laugh at that.

During one of my early visits to Uncle Wilfred's, I complained of a sore left ear. Aunt Ada checked it and discovered a large boil at the entrance to the ear canal where she couldn't prick it with a needle or squeeze it with her fingers. When Wilfred came into the kitchen, he examined it and asked Ada to get the fountain pen from the sideboard. He told me to lie down on the kitchen couch with the sore ear up. He held my head down with one big hand and pressed the smooth rounded end of the pen hard against the ear beside the boil. I screamed, and the boil popped like a gunshot. Aunt Ada moved in and cleaned up the mess with tissue, alcohol and iodine. After a short rest, I got up feeling as good as new.

Barney and Me

Wilfred and Ada had four children. The eldest daughter was grown up and gone by the time I got there. The eldest son, Douglas, or 'Buddy', was in his late teens and eventually became my mentor. Frances, in her early teens, was the next daughter, and Carl was the youngest. He was just a bit younger than me, and we had some fun times together. The farm overlooked Savage Harbour and the bay with mostly clear fields and a small clump of bush down by the water.

I'll never forget those summers at Uncle Wilfred's, being accepted and treated as part of the family, with all kinds of good-natured teasing to get a rise out of me. We were fed like kings by Ada and her mom Gertie, who never seemed to stop baking and cooking and serving three meals a day for family, relatives home from away, visitors, and hired hands working on the farm.

At mealtime, Carl and I sat on two small hardwood chairs at the far end of the dining room table where the ladies of the house fondly referred to us as "those two hungry buggers". It was a great spot for us except we depended on others at the table to pass food to us, and when we finished gulping down our food ahead of everyone else, we had to sit there and behave until the rest of them finished eating and left the table.

Ada and her mom had a rule for youngsters and some adults that when we were called to come and get it, we first had to wash our hands, then sit or lie down and relax for at least five minutes to cool off before we ate, and the same afterwards, so we wouldn't get cramps.

When we were small, Carl and I ran little chores and errands to help the ladies, like taking cold water or messages to the men in the field and taking empty containers and messages back to the house. We also fed the hens and gathered the eggs, and for at least two summers we bottle-fed lambs that had been orphaned by mothers that died giving them birth or had been left hungry by mothers that simply refused to feed their own. Aunt Ada rigged up some large pop bottles with baby's nipples on them so we could feed the lambs with cow's skim milk every morning and evening after the milking and separating were done.

One summer there were three orphaned lambs and, like the others, they became pets. One had a white face, so we named it Whitey. Another had a black face and was uglier than the others, so we named it Blackie. The third was bigger, a ram that would latch onto the bottle and not let go until it was empty, so we called him Hungry. Blackie and Whitey grew up to be mothers, and Hungry was sold in the fall as a cash crop. Carl later told me that every spring Whitey had twin lambs and Blackie only had a single.

As soon as I was old enough to help in the fields, I went on the hay wagon to help Wilfred build the loads. All the hay was cut by a team of horses pulling a mower, raked by a single horse with a dump rake, and stacked in small coils in bulk in the field. There were no hay balers.

Barney and Me

Once Wilfred was confident that I could build a load alone and drive the team from coil to coil in the field, he let me do it. I had to receive the loose hay from the men on the ground, distribute it on the wagon and tramp it down so it wouldn't fall off on its way to the barn. Buddy and a hired man named Charlie would walk beside the wagon, one on each side, and would throw the hay up to me using hand-held pitch forks with extra long handles.

Charlie was a major tease. He'd wait for Buddy to throw a pitch up to me and for me to turn my back to catch it. Then Charlie would load his fork with all the hay he could gather and holler to me, "Are ya up there?" At the same time that fork full of hay would land on my back. I'd sputter and cough and call him all the nasty names I could lay my tongue on, and he'd almost roll on the ground laughing. Buddy would also get a good chuckle out of it. This wasn't an isolated incident. It might occur two or three times during a load, and there were five or six loads a day, if the weather held.

A standing rule on the farm was, "He who builds the load drives the horses back to the barn." Others had to walk or hang onto the back of the wagon. One summer, the old wooden wheel truck wagon with a 'V' frame on it was replaced by a nearly new rubber tired truck wagon made from the chassis of an old car. Wilfred and Buddy built a new Western frame on it that was much easier for building loads due to the wide, flat deck and the high, square ends. It even had a post high in the center of the front rack that I could tie the reins to, so they wouldn't fall down around the horses' feet and spook them. That's where I learned to tie two half hitches.

One afternoon I was building the load on this new wagon in the lighthouse field when it started to rain. I had almost a full load of hay on, and about ten feet above the ground when Buddy told me to head for the barn. I had Jack and Dell hooked to the wagon, and they both loved to run. I turned them out of the field out onto the lane and chirped to them. We came up the lane at a good clip, and I kept a tight rein on them all the way. Wilfred was standing in the yard and saw us coming. When we went by the end of the house and crossed the drain pipe from the kitchen sink, the load bounced and started to shift to the right. I held the reins in my left hand, grabbed my pitch fork in the other and jumped with the falling hay. I hollered, "Whoa," and the team slowed and stopped. I landed on the ground standing on both feet, knee deep in hay beside the wagon, still holding the reins in one hand and the fork in the other. Wilfred later said, "I never before saw anything like it." He was so impressed that he never scolded me for driving too fast. He just went to the barn and brought his horse Beauty to the yard with the big pitch fork attached, stuck the fork into the hay on the ground and dragged it to the loft door where it could be pulled up into the mow.

Afterwards, Wilfred brought Beauty around to the other end of the barn for me to hook her onto the hay rope that lifted the hay off the wagon up into the loft and onto a steel track that was suspended from the rafters. Here I resumed my other job, driving Beauty as she pulled the rope that hoisted the hay into the loft. She was strong and obedient, anything but a Beauty. On an "okay" from Buddy at the other end of the barn, I started off slow at first, holding the loose rope so the swing wouldn't hit Beauty on the heels. When the rope tightened, I stepped up beside the horse and urged her on until I heard Buddy holler, "Whoa." I moved beside her for two reasons. One was that if the tight rope snapped during the pull and I was close to it, it might cut me in half or seriously injure me. The other reason was that Beauty had the nasty habit of squirting urine when she was over-extended. Walking behind her was no place to be.

The pull on the hay rope lasted less than a minute, and we might travel thirty some yards in a straight line. Each time, at the end of the pull, I had to unhook the hay rope off the swing so that Buddy could pull it back for the next lift. I'd then pick up the sometimes urine-covered swing with one hand (no gloves) and pull back on it so that Beauty wouldn't get tangled in the traces as I steered her back for the next lift. I repeated this maneuver until the wagon was unloaded, then unhitched Beauty and tied her in the shade until we came back from the field with the next load. As a teenager, I did that job for several summers, and when I got tough enough, I joined the crew that stowed the hay in the loft. Now, there's an unforgettable job on a hot, humid summer afternoon, sweating profusely and inhaling the dust.

My time at Wilfred's wasn't all work. If Aunt Ada had time after supper she would take Carl and me in the car to the North Shore where we could bathe in small pools of warm water and get cleaned up after a day on the farm. During free time, I learned to ride Dell bareback. What a thrill it was galloping down the lane or across the fields as fast as she could go with the wind blowing through my hair. It was as smooth as sitting in a rocking chair.

Some evenings when we were running late, Wilfred would ask me to jump on Dell's back and go bring the cows home from the pasture for milking. Dell wore only her bridle and a short piece of rope to steer her. I galloped her down the farm lane to the pasture gate that consisted of two or three wooden rails suspended on crossbars between two small posts on each side of the lane. I'd pull Dell up beside the rails, reach down and slide the two top rails to one side and drop the ends on the ground, then I'd circle Dell back into the lane, point her toward the pasture, and chirp to her. She'd lunge forward, jump the bottom rail and keep going until we found the cows. We'd round them up and walk them back through the gate out into the lane. I'd jump down off Dell, hold the reins in one hand and put the rails up with the other. Then I'd climb up onto her back and drive the cows slowly to the barn so as to not get them overheated before milking.

Buddy and others would steer the cows into their stalls and tie them there.

After I put Dell in her stall in the horse stable and took her bridle off, I'd go to the cow stable to help with the milking, which was done by hand into stainless steel buckets. When that was finished, I might take a turn at cranking the handle on the separator that separated the cream from the skim milk, which we fed directly to the calves in pens or in a nearby field, to the orphaned lambs, to the pigs and to the barn cats and kittens.

Such was the daily life in summer at Wilfred's farm and every other family farm on the Island in those days. I was proud and privileged to be a part of it, and I believe I'm a better person for it.

Me working a hay wagon

Dad's last horses – Maude, Queen, and my horse Dell

Chapter 17

The Forge

In the 1940s and 50s, on farms and in the woods and around the shores of P.E.I., horses were still the primary source for driving power and winter travel. They had to be fit for all their tasks, and one basic element was the condition of their feet. Hence, during those years, there were no less than three forges or blacksmith shops in our village. One, Alden's, was so close to my house that Donald and I could wake each weekday morning to the ring of the hammer on the anvil. The driveway from both our back yards to the river went past the forge, and only a narrow street separated it from the river. We rarely ever went by it without 'droppin in to see what was goin on'.

Donald and I were almost always welcome. In summer the doors would be wide open and we could easily see and hear everything. In winter on a stormy day they'd be closed, but we knew how to open them and go in. Alden might be just lighting the fire in the hearth, or he might already be building or repairing some tool or piece of machinery. He might be putting a set of new shoes on a horse or just repairing a broken or bent one. The customer might still be there or he might have dropped the item or the horse off and gone shopping across the bridge.

There was plenty of demand for blacksmithing. If a horse needed shoeing, we took it to the forge. If a wagon wheel needed fixing or a new steel rim, we took it to the forge. If a plough shear or any other piece of machinery broke, we took it to the forge. On rainy days when farmers couldn't work on the land, the forge was usually a busy place. Some days in winter, teams of horses would be lined up outside waiting to be shod, or as they say in Ontario, "to have their shoes sharpened or replaced."

On these days Alden would have a helper, sometimes his brother Ira. On other days he would be alone, and Donald or I would be asked to pass him something or hold something because his two hands just weren't enough. We were always warned to be careful, especially around hot steel that didn't look hot but could give a severe burn. We already knew that some horses would kick worse than others, but we were still warned to keep our distance.

Like all forges of the day, Alden's had a fire box that burned a special blacksmith coal. It was a fine coal, almost a powder, that would burn hotter and generate more heat for a longer time than ordinary coal. Plumbed into the base of the firebox was a pipe that brought forced

air in below the fire from a large bellows that was suspended on a wooden frame. Above the bellows was a long
wooden handle attached to the wide end and pivoted on
the frame above it. The business end of the handle was
conveniently available to the blacksmith where he stood
by the fire box, so he could pump air into the fire as
needed. At the same time, with his other hand, he could
stir the fire with a poker or a pair of tongs that he had
made himself. Later on, when electricity came to the
village, Alden replaced the big, old hand bellows with
an electric motor that had a blower on it, which is common today but was a wonderful invention in that time.
Around the same time, Alden installed an electric motor
and a V-belt on his drill press, which up until then was
hand operated. These conveniences surely made his job
a lot easier.

Another valuable accessory in the forge was a small
wooden tub that sat on the floor in front of the anvil
with water in it. This was where Alden dunked hot steel
to cool it off after he was finished shaping it. The rim
of the tub bore the scars of hot metal, especially horse
shoes being left to hang there while they cooled enough
to be touched. The tub was also a quick source of water
if a wayward spark started a fire in the mostly wooden
building.

Each time a piece of hot steel came out of the fire,
it was placed on top of the anvil to be shaped by the
blacksmith with his hammer. When he'd strike the hot

steel with his hammer, the sparks would fly, especially if there was welding powder on it. He applied this powder with an old tablespoon before the red hot object was returned to the fire, then brought it back out in about ten seconds to weld one piece of steel to another, the same as a welder might do today.

To say that the anvil was vital to the operation of the forge would be minimizing its importance, as almost everything passed over it. It had a flat upper surface on the right hand side and a large horn on the left. There was a square hole in the right hand end that held attachments such as an inverted chisel that allowed Alden to cut pieces of metal, cold or hot, by holding them over it and striking them with a hammer. There was also a small round hole near the square hole that was used to hold hot, round pieces of steel so they could be easily bent or shaped before they cooled. He would usually hold these objects with a pair of tongs, one of a selection he had made himself, depending on the task at hand.

Some said the anvil weighed in excess of 200 pounds, and it was often the object of labor-toughened young men wanting to show off their superior strength. With Alden's approval, they would try to lift it off the wooden block and hold it, just for a moment. Many of them could, much to the pleasure of the bystanders.

As I mentioned earlier, if Alden needed to fasten two pieces of steel together or to put a calk on a horseshoe, he would first heat the two pieces until they were red hot, take them out of the fire, sprinkle some welding powder on the joint, return them to the fire for a few seconds, bring them back out, place the two pieces together on the anvil, hold them steady, and strike the joint with the hammer to initially tack it. Then he would turn the new piece over to inspect it for accuracy and at the same time tap the new joint with the hammer to shape it to the desired form. If the object cooled during this process, he would return it to the fire, heat it up until red, return it to the anvil and complete the task to his satisfaction.

During the initial union, if the two pieces to be joined were too large or too long for one man to maneuver, that's where sometimes Donald or I would step in and grab a pair of tongs to hold one piece until the connection was made. This situation was common during the welding of a long piece of flat iron that had been put through a set of rollers to create a circle to become a steel shoe for a wooden wagon wheel. The weld for this operation was difficult because of the spring effect in the steel and its resistance to being forced together. Here again an extra pair of hands came in handy.

Prior to this, the wooden wheel may have required repairs to either the rim or the spokes. Alden was quite capable at working with wood and had the tools to do the job. Once the wheel had been repaired and the steel shoe welded, then came the task of heating the steel to expand it enough so it would fit onto the wheel. This again is where Donald and I might be asked to help by cutting up short pieces of kindling and placing them on end around the shoe inside and out, which by now was lying on its side on four bricks to keep it off the ground and let the burning wood have the greatest effect. Alden would set the receiving wheel also on the ground on bricks nearby so that when the shoe was heated enough to expand the transfer could be made quickly. He had special, long handled tongs and usually needed help to complete the task. None of this would be attempted unless the day was fine and the wind was right. Alden would pour some oil or gasoline on the kindling and light it. When the red coals burned down, the hot shoe was lifted onto the wooden wheel and forced into position. The hot steel would scorch the wood and sometimes ignite it so we always needed a bucket of water nearby. When the steel cooled, it contracted and made a nice fit on the wooden wheel, good for many more safe miles and heavy loads.

A more common task of the blacksmith was shoeing horses. This involved getting acquainted with the horse, making it comfortable and persuading it to pick up its foot when he reached for it. If there was an old shoe on the foot, it had to be pulled off with a special pair of tongs. Then the hoof had to be trimmed and shaped to make ready for the new shoe. This was a craft unto itself, and had to be repeated three times if all four hooves were to be shod.

Blank horseshoes came in all sizes from a supplier in the city and had to be modified to suit the horse's hoof and its working conditions. The new shoe had to be heated, modified and shaped to fit the individual hoof. Hopefully it was the right size to begin with and the correct shoe for the foot, because front horse shoes are different from back shoes.

In winter, a major modification was the addition of calks to prevent the horse from slipping on ice. The two calks on the back of the shoe were usually fashioned by heating and bending the back tips of the shoe down and heating and sharpening them with the hammer on the anvil. The calk for the front of the shoe was a separate, similar piece of steel, heated, sharpened and welded in place. Each shoe had to be fitted and nailed to the intended hoof using special horseshoe nails for the purpose, six or eight nails, depending on the number of holes in the shoe. After all this, the horse would be good to go. Now the driver had to be extra careful in deep snow to keep the horse from cutting his legs with his newly sharpened shoes.

The nails for the shoes were slim and tapered on one side so they would go toward the outside of the hoof, not into the hoof. This takes much practice and skill. If a nail does start into the hoof wrongly, it has to be pulled and discarded because of pain to the horse and possible infection. When the nails are all in place and the shoe is secure, the tips have to be cut off. The ends then need to be clinched down outside the hoof and filed with a rasp so that no sharps edges remain. All work is done with the horse's hoof either between the smitty's knees or on a special stand designed for the purpose.

Donald and I were forever fascinated by 'all the goins-on' at the forge and, as young boys are want to do, we dreamed that some day we too could be blacksmiths. Donald specifically recalls that on one of our trips to the slaughter house, we came home with two cows' feet with part of the leg still attached. We borrowed two used horseshoes from Alden with some old nails that we straightened and proceeded to nail the shoes onto the cow's feet. We found out the hard way that shoeing was not nearly as easy as it looked. Little did we know what the future held for horses and buggies with the advent of many more automobiles and farm tractors in the decade that followed.

When Donald and I first hit the road and started visiting neighbours, one of our first and frequent calls was to see Jean, who was Alden the blacksmith's wife. She was a beautiful young bride with an infectious laugh and smile who always made Donald and me feel welcome. She also baked great cookies. She and Alden lived in Winston Birt's house across the street from the telephone office where Donald lived, so we didn't have far to go. To me, it didn't hurt that her maiden name was Jay.

Another major attraction at Jean's house was their dog Lassie. Lassie was a water spaniel who loved to swim and fetch sticks that we'd throw into the river. In the fall, she'd also go duck hunting with Alden and his friends.

Jean even took a picture of Donald, Lassie and me sitting on the ground in her backyard, which is on the front cover of this book. Lassie's face isn't visible because she was camera shy and turned her back to the camera.

One day, after Alden and Jean moved over to Mac-Gregor's house beside Donald's place and closer to the forge, Donald and I visited Jean in her kitchen. When she asked us, "What's new, and who did you see lately?" we mentioned seeing Donald's cousin Ramona and her friend Amy all dressed up coming from church. Donald said they both were wearing perfume and lipstick, and I blurted out that Amy had nice legs. Jean pounced on my remark and said, "Oh, really, and what were you doing looking at Amy's legs?" I got as as red as a beet, started stammering, and made some feeble excuse that her seam wasn't straight on her nylons. Jean almost doubled over with laughter, then took mercy on me, patted me on the shoulder, and said, "It's okay Allison. I'm sorry," but for the longest time afterward, she took great pleasure teasing me about looking at Amy's legs.

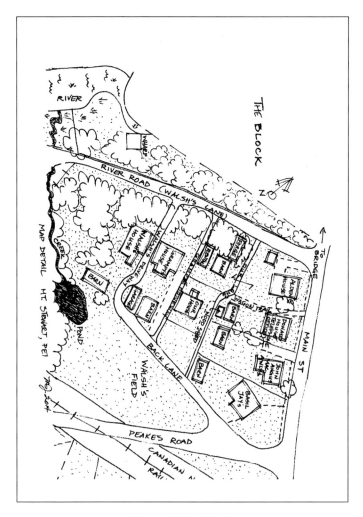

Map of The Block

Chapter 18

The Block

In the mid 1940s as we walked or drove across the bridge from the business side of the village in a southerly direction, the first house we came to after River Road was a brown two storey home occupied by Alex MacGregor and his wife. They rented the second floor to Freeman Affleck and his wife after he returned with his war bride.

The next house on the right was the telephone office, a duplex owned and occupied by Donald's family on one side and Ma's sister Ellie and her brother Danny on the other. Ma, the Matriarch, was grandmother to Donald and his three sisters. The house was two stories with a sun porch on the front, right beside the sidewalk. It had a large back yard with a small barn and an outside toilet.

The next house on the right hand side was John Angus MacAulay's, another smaller two-storey house, where he and his wife, both seniors, lived. They didn't have any children. They had a large back yard and a bigger barn than Donald's family. Donald recalls the day that John Angus died in his toilet inside the barn, and Ma helped

Mrs. MacAulay carry him into the house.

The next house on the same side on the corner of Main Street and Peakes Road was owned by Basil Jay and family. It was a small two-storey home with a long back yard and an equally long barn that ran beside the back lane leading into our place. That house was almost surrounded by mature lilac bushes laden with flowers each spring. Basil used the front part of the barn as a garage where he did mechanical work. The back lane was the only access to the parking lot in front of our house and to the barn and the woodshed beyond.

Our house was a two-storey double tenement that housed our family on the left side and Little Alex MacDonald's family on the right hand side. It and the next two houses to the West had been built in the mid to late 1800s by out-of-work ship builders from one of the several shipyards of the day.

Returning to the entrance of the River Road and heading along it, in MacGregor's back yard, was a small building with a cellar to keep food cool in summer, and next to it across a laneway was Alden's forge. Next came the driveway to Grampy's two-storey rental, which he had built himself and which partially blocked our view of the river. Then came Grampy's front driveway beside his large front lawn and large two-storey double tenement occupied by Grampy and his wife Jennie on one side and by Mrs. Cummiskey, a school teacher, and her two daughters on the other.

Barney and Me

The last home on the block was Walsh's, occupied by two spinster sisters, Evelyn and Helen, until their brother Reggie returned home from the War and joined them. Theirs was a large property with trees, gardens, a barn and a separate garage for the family car. Their laneway, like Grampy's, ran from the river at the front all the way through to the back lane. That property also had a small field with a pond behind the barn and a spring in the corner by the railroad that fed the pond, a place for neighbourhood children to play ball in summer and skate in winter. After Reggie returned home, the field was usually occupied in summer by his horse Tom, to which all the children became quite attached, especially Donald and I. We would run out the lane to meet Tom and Reggie so we could hitch short rides on the wagon in summer and on the wood sleigh in winter as Reggie returned from his small farm in Cherry Hill.

Most of the properties in The Block were separated by barns and fences, some rather fancy with turned posts and special ornamental wire, but many fences were simply high board fences that had to be whitewashed with lime every spring to make them look nice for the summer. When I got old enough, I did my share of whitewashing board fences and then some.

We all have many memories, mostly fond, of The Block and our time there. My two younger sisters were born there.

Donald and me with family on Walsh's Pond

Donald with children from The Block

Chapter 19

Walsh's Pond

Of all our favourite haunts during our boyhood days, Walsh's pond ranked right up there with the best, in all seasons. This was for many reasons, not the least of which was proximity to our homes. A strong arm could throw a rock into the pond from our front parking lot. It was at the South-west end of Walsh's field, which was directly in front of our house. The pie-shaped field and the pond were between our back lane and the railway track, and they totaled no more than two acres. Another major reason was, although the land was privately owned by two spinster sisters and their bachelor brother Reggie, we were never stopped from entering unless the gate was closed and Tom the horse was in it. That was the case with all the children on the block. We were all welcome!

In winter, when the ice was fit, we skated on the pond between the bull rushes and the hummocks. Many of us took our first few strides on skates and falls on our asses there, but eventually learned to skate a little bit. Donald and I would also visit the small spring fed well in the corner of the pond next to the field and the railway track. When it finally froze over, the ice was transparent and it was like looking through the glass into an aquarium, although we never even knew such a thing existed. Some winters hibernating frogs would be visible upside down with their white bellies showing, frozen into the ice.

One winter, to help a young neighbour mother whose husband was away working, I offered to take her five year old son to teach him how to skate. I took along an old wooden kitchen chair with no back on it so he could push it in front of him to help keep his balance. He got along pretty well, with just a few falls away from the chair, but one time he fell forward into the edge of the chair seat and put his front teeth through his lower lip. He cried and bled, and I tried to console him, picked him up and carried him back to his mom. She was cordial about the whole thing, but neither the mother nor the son asked me to go again. The boy survived and didn't seem to hate me afterwards. Much later, on my first vacation back home in March, Donald and I took our younger sisters to skate and play on the pond, just for old time's sake.

In spring, when the well thawed out, a jelly-like mass of frog's eggs, about the size of a hand, would appear in the water. We'd try to pick them up, but they were too slippery. We were careful not to break them. Later, when the eggs hatched, a collection of polly wogs wiggled in the water, and before long some of them became baby frogs. At times like this curiosity compelled Donald and

I to visit the well almost every day.

Spring also brought a vibrant growth of plant life, like marsh marigolds, water lilies and purple flowers, which we later learned were irises. At that time we could see the early formation of what we called bull rushes and later learned to be cattails.

Also, on one of the hummocks in the pond would appear at least one black duck's nest, noticeable by the traffic of the nesting pair. Later, the female would sit on her eggs to hatch, while the drake stood guard. Donald and I had strict orders not to disturb the duck while she was nesting. Later in the spring we were really excited to see the mother appear on the pond with five or six baby ducks swimming behind her.

At another time, Donald and I would go 'jumpin the hummocks' in the pond, trying not to slip off and get our feet wet. Sometimes, we didn't succeed.

The pond was drained by a small deep brook that ran to the river, not much more than a foot wide in places. It ran down beside Walsh's yard, away from the house, on the other side of a row of small spruce, outside the perimeter yard fence. Donald and I found this to be an excellent hideaway, where we could sit on the bank in the sun with our backs to the trees, take our sneakers off and soak our feet in the brook. It was also one of our prime spots to go to have a smoke undetected, except for Ernest's cows staring at us from behind the fence on the other side of the brook.

One day, we mused about putting a water wheel in the brook. We had heard of someone who made an ornamental water wheel out of a small fir tree, so we went to the woods and found one. We fashioned it with our pocket knives so that the stem of the tree with the top and bottom cut off was the axis on which it could turn. We cut the middle branches off the stem, brought the bottom row of branches up, and tied them to the top of the stem with binder twine. Those bow-like branches created paddles that dipped into the water when the unit was suspended on two 'Y' shaped sticks driven into the ground on either side of the brook. We chose the top of the only little waterfall in the brook for its location. After some adjustments, the moving water turned the wheel, and we were overjoyed. In the evening we left it running and went home. When we returned the next day, one of the branches had broken free and the wheel had stalled. We tried to fix it but the damage was too severe, so we dismantled it and went home.

In the fall when the cattails matured, Donald and I would cut five or six of the best of them, take them home, and soak the heads in a large can of fuel oil overnight. The following evening after dark, we would light two of them with wooden matches, and chase the girls around the yards to make them scream. After a while we'd light the rest of the torches, give them all to the girls and let them chase us.

Later in the fall or early winter, when the heads of

the remaining cat tails became fluffy, we'd cut them off and chase the girls with them. When we got hit with the fluffs from a cattail, they got in our hair and all over our clothes. The good news was that the wind blew most of the fluffs away.

The forge, Grampy Jay's house, and Walsh's house

Construction on the Mount Stewart bridge

Chapter 20

The New Mount Stewart Bridge

In the late 1940s, after World War Two, when I was about ten and Donald was nine, the P.E.I. Department of Highways decided to replace the old span in the Mount Stewart bridge. It had become dilapidated and unsafe. The approach from both sides was a causeway which needed some shoring-up on the sides with large rocks, but otherwise was okay. The main repair was to the span in the middle where the river ran under it. During the demolition and reconstruction all vehicle and horse traffic was rerouted five miles around the head of the river, and foot traffic used the railway bridge two hundred yards up river. When the old span was torn out it left a gaping hole where Donald and I could peek down at the rushing water on the changing tides, though the workmen warned us to keep our distance for safety sake. We were like a couple of inspectors checking on the daily progress of the job, and as the workmen got to know us, they would kid with us and tell us stories that seemed, even to us, to stretch the truth, just to get our reaction.

One story was about a lobster eating contest in She-diac, New Brunswick earlier that year where Joe told us he beat Mickey by eating seventeen market-sized lobsters, while Mickey could only manage to eat fourteen. We listened, but we didn't believe them. They also told us what they would do to us if we broke anything while we were there. We just laughed at them because we knew that they went home every night and that there was no night watchman if we were inclined to do anything bad. But, we didn't.

The new span was to be set on large creosote pilings that looked like inverted telephone poles. They were brought in on an extra long trailer, and the men had to attach a sharp pointed steel shoe to the small end of each one. This was to help the piling penetrate the mud and clay in the river bed below. On the large end of each piling the men fastened a steel band to prevent the pile driver from damaging it as it was being driven into the river bed. The pile driver consisted of a large wooden structure with a tower and a steam engine that hoisted a big steel block up the tower on a track as high as it would go. When the block was lined up above the piling, the operator would release it, and it came down on the large end of the piling with a loud "thump". Donald and I could see the piling sink into the water a few inches with every thump. This would be repeated many times until the piling reached the desired depth. The operation continued day after day until all the pilings were in place.

When the pilings were secure on both sides of the river, large creosote timbers were fastened to the middle and top of them to reinforce the structure. When the span arrived, it consisted of two used flat-bed railway cars with the wheels, axles and couplers removed. They were hoisted into place by a giant steam powered crane, with the ends resting on the new creosote structure on both sides of the river. Once secure, a wooden and steel deck was built on top of and between them to hold the concrete deck that would later become the traffic surface of the new span. Provision was also made for a sidewalk on one side of the span.

There were no ready-mix trucks then, so all the concrete had to be mixed in a barrel mixer driven by a small gasoline engine and then pushed to its destination in wheel barrows over a road of wooden planks. To provide for sockets that would eventually hold the railings at the side of the bridge, empty wine bottles were inserted into the wet concrete. When the concrete hardened, the bottles were broken and the railings attached. Other wine bottles were also placed on the outside edges of the span to allow for drainage of surface water. After two or three months of hard work, the new span was completed and opened to traffic.

About that time, Donald and I had become quite proficient at 'cussin and swearin', and the workmen on the bridge may have added a few new expletives to our collection. I don't know what Donald did about this bad habit at home, but I could be cussing outside and the minute I crossed the doorstep into our house the 'off switch' activated, and I never swore in the house.

I was proud that I was doing well in that department, but I failed to allow for two other habits that I had. One was that I sometimes had nightmares, and the other was that I talked in my sleep. So one night, when everyone in the house was fast asleep, including me, Mom, who never swore in her life, was awakened by a ruckus coming from my bedroom. It was me shouting and cussing at somebody. She dragged herself out of bed, walked half-asleep out into the hall and stood at my bedroom door, appalled at what was coming from the mouth of her fair-haired only son. She said later that I stopped shortly after she got there. She didn't wake me but turned and went back to bed in disbelief and disappointment. She probably had some difficulty getting back to sleep that night.

A couple of days later, when she and I were alone, she recounted what she had heard that night and asked if it was a common practice of mine when I was away from home. I assured her that I only swore when I was playing with other boys who swore at me first, which may not have been the exact truth. I felt terrible about Mom having to experience my foul mouth and tried to curb this habit with some success. I made sure I never swore in her presence again, asleep or awake.

Later, I told Donald about my Mom catching me

swearing in my sleep. He chuckled and said, "From now on I'm gonna have to watch my tongue when I'm in our house and yours too."

Clark's store

Chapter 21

Stores of the Village

When we were young, all the stores in the village were on the North side of the river and all except one, Clark's, were on the East side of Main Street Owned and operated by Russie Clark, Clark's was the biggest and carried a greater variety of supplies than any other store in the village. They had everything from needles and thread to bags of flour and animal feed. They sold everything a family might need – boots, shoes and clothing for all ages, for work and play and Sunday-go-to-meeting clothes. The ground floor had groceries and dry goods, mostly in bins and on shelves from floor to ceiling. The clerks used a long pole with a clamp on the end to reach for lighter items on the top shelf. Once a week, customers from the country could drop off their grocery lists and go visiting or to an appointment. Their orders would be filled, waiting for them when they returned. If their funds were low, they could get their order on credit and pay for it later when their cash flow improved.

Items such as kerosene and molasses were kept in

bulk in the back of the store, and customers brought in their empty gallon cans or glass jars and got them filled. Kerosene came in a metal drum and was gravity fed from an elevated stand. Molasses came in a ninety gallon wooden puncheon which had a crank pump inserted on top to deliver the molasses to the receptacle.

Upstairs in the store were blankets and bedding, window blinds and curtains, nuts and bolts, spikes and nails, also flat steel to make runners for sleighs and wagon wheels. They even had caskets and rough boxes for burials. If you needed something from the second floor, you were accompanied there by a clerk. Back downstairs, small items would go into paper bags, while larger items were wrapped in heavy brown paper from a roll mounted on the end of the main sales counter. The roll had a weighted cutting bar on top, so when the clerk had the desired length of paper, a quick tug sideways with both hands severed it from the roll. The package was then wrapped and tied with string from a ball sitting high on a shelf and threaded through eyes mounted on the ceiling, so the string hung down over the packing station. Butcher shops had a similar roll of brown paper, but it was waxed on the inside to prevent the meat juices from seeping through it.

Outside in front of the store, almost on the street, was a gasoline pump, the kind that had a large glass tank on top into which the clerk pumped the gas from the underground tank. The glass tank was marked off in gallons, so if a customer wanted two gallons, the clerk stopped pumping at that point, put the filling hose nozzle into the gas tank of the vehicle, and the gas was gravity fed into the tank.

Across the street was Clark's Meat Store, operated by Harold Affleck, the butcher. When he joined his brother Bruce to open Affleck Bros. store further up the street, Alden Birt, the former blacksmith, took over the operation of Clark's Meat Store. This was the store where one of my older sisters or I went every morning before school to get something for dinner. Mom would give us money from the sugar bowl in the kitchen cupboard that Daddy had left there when he was home on the weekend. Mom cooked whatever meat we got at the store plus vegetables that morning. We came home at Noon, had our dinner and went back to school in an hour. We had less than two city blocks to walk each way.

Ma, Donald's grandmother, had a standing invitation from Affleck's that whenever a beef was to be butchered, Harold or Bruce would call, and she would send one of the children over to get some blood. She sent a huge rectangular cake pan with whomever volunteered. Donald and I would occasionally be conscripted. We had to be there before the animal was killed so the butcher could catch the blood before it spilled on the floor.

We usually arrived while the animal was still standing. It would be tethered with a rope on its horns that was tied to rings on the side walls so it couldn't swing its head. Ted Garnhum used a small sledge hammer to strike a fatal blow to the forehead, right between the eyes. The target was the center of an imaginary 'X' formed by two lines, one from the right horn to the left eye and one from the left horn to the right eye.

When the animal fell, two meat hooks were inserted into the hind legs just above the hocks. The hooks would then be fastened to a block and tackle suspended from the ceiling, and the animal would be manually hauled up, rear end first, until the nose cleared the floor. The butcher would then slit its throat and catch some of the blood for us in Ma's cake pan. The rest would be saved in tubs or buckets.

Now Donald and I would head back home across the bridge, taking turns carrying the cake pan and trying our best not to spill any. At home, Ma would add spices and onions and bake it in the oven in the same pan. She called it blood pudding. Not really 'hankerin' to eat blood, I would decline the invitation to stay for dinner, but I'm sure Donald and his family enjoyed it.

It was outside Clarke's store one morning that I was confronted by the village bully who was lying in wait to accuse me of saying nasty things about him. I was only about ten years old, and he was bigger and meaner than me. I almost wet my pants. He grabbed me, but as good luck would have it, Lester came out of the store and separated us before any blows were struck. He told us both to get going, which we did, in different directions, thankfully. I learned later that some older boys had put Pete up to it by filling his head full of lies.

Clark's also had two branch stores, one in Montague, about twenty miles Southeast, operated by Russie's son Kier, and one in St. Peters, about the same distance Northeast, operated by his son Sterling. By the standards of the day, Clark's was a rural commercial empire. They would sell seed and fertilizer to farmers in the spring on tick and buy back potatoes, grain and other products in the fall, at their price. They ran their own herd of beef cattle on the farm near the village as well as others on farms outside the village. They had their own small fleet of five ton straight trucks, all with sides made of stakes to haul cattle. These racks could be removed to carry lumber, hay or other bulky product.

On the main farm, at the top of the Back Street, Clark's had a large warehouse for storing potatoes in the fall and grading and shipping them during the winter. The warehouse had its own railway siding as the Georgetown line ran right past it.

Beside the main store in the village and South towards the river was another building that served as a warehouse for surplus product for the three stores as well as for animal feed, fencing supplies and anything else a farmer might need. At the back of the property behind this building was a covered wagon shed where customers could tie their horses out of the weather.

Going North on the same side of the street as Clark's

Barney and Me

Meat store, just past the entrance to the Back Street, was Billy MacLeod's general store. It carried clothing, footwear, groceries, some hardware, but of considerably less volume than Clark's. Billy also had a gas pump outside in front of his store right beside the sidewalk. It had a glass dome Esso sign on top that lit up at night. Billy and his family lived in a big house on the Back Street, just behind the store. He also had hitching posts for customers' horses beside the Back Street across from the store.

Further North on the same side of the Main Street was Luther Coffin's house. It had a one room shop with a big front window that for a time was home to the village cobbler.

The next building North was the store of MacLeod Douglas, aka 'Scuddy', specializing in confectionery, a wide variety of bulk candy in showcases, fresh fruit when he could get it, soda pop, potato chips, some dry goods and canned goods. Bananas came complete with the stalk, which was suspended by a rope from the ceiling and bunches could be cut off as the customer needed. On Saturday nights, this was the place to hang out, stand around, listen to the adults tell stories, tease each other and enjoy a treat. Donald and I had a choice of Seaman's Orange pop, Lime Rickey, Pepsi, Coca Cola, or Ginger Ale for five cents if we drank it there, seven cents if we took it out, but we could get our two cents back when we returned the empty bottle. Potato chips, ice cream cones, popsicles, Artic bars or chocolate dips were all five cents. The only question was how much money we had and how much of it we wanted to spend.

Next door to the Douglas store was Feehan's General Gtore, operated by Adrian Feehan and by his father Felix before him. It carried supplies similar to Clark's but with less volume and selection. Like Clarks, Feehan's store had a covered wagon shed out back for customers' horses during the week and for church goers on Sunday.

Daddy told the story that one winter Sunday morning, when we still lived in Fanningbrook, he drove my horse Dell to Mount Stewart alone in the box sleigh, tied and rugged her in Feehan's shed while he went to church. When he came to get Dell after church, her rug wasn't on her, and she was standing there with the steam coming off her. He examined her and concluded that someone had given her an awful trip somewhere and back in the hour that he was in church. Dell was so weak that she could hardly back the sleigh out of the shed, and she was unable to hold her head up. He didn't get into the sleigh but walked beside her all the way home, sometimes holding her head up to keep her nose from dragging on the ground. It took her days after to recover from that trip. Daddy found out later that some teenage boys from the village had borrowed her to go down the river two or three miles to get some moonshine. It sickened him more to learn that one of them was a Jay.

North past a couple of houses on the same side of

the street was Affleck Bros. Butcher Shop and Grocery with a slaughter house out back. As I said earlier, it was operated by Harold and Bruce Affleck. My uncle Wilfred, a farmer from Savage Harbour, six miles to the Northeast, sold them a fatted steer each year for their Easter beef. It was usually delivered by my uncle and his eldest son Buddy in a large crate on a wood sleigh pulled by a team of horses consisting of my mare Dell and her partner Jack. If I knew they were coming and I was around, Donald and I would run to meet them at the North end of the village and ride in with them. If there was not enough snow on the ground for a sleigh, then the team would be pulling a truck wagon.

A bit further up the street was a small meat and fish market operated initially by Pius Griffin and later by Ray Gallagher when Pius moved to Nova Scotia.

Continuing North past a house and a set of railway tracks across Main Street from the railway station was the Co-op general store managed by Jimmy Doyle. It was known to some of the residents as the 'Coop' by the way it was spelled. That store, like Feehan's, carried a similar selection of goods to Clark's only on a smaller scale. Donald and I rarely went to that store. The Co-op store had a small warehouse beside it that held items too large to keep in the store. Behind the store some distance East was the Co-op saw mill that I've mentioned later in this edition.

Chapter 22

Trucks

Some of the men who returned from World War Two invested in trucks and set about finding work for them. Art Doyle, who never drank liquor or smoked, bought a new three ton Ford, navy blue in color, that had a flat bed with a stake body to haul bulky loads. One of his early jobs was hauling cases of jam from the strawberry cannery to outlets in Nova Scotia. Later, during the strawberry season, he switched to a reefer box, to haul fresh strawberries to Boston, a distance of seven hundred miles. Inside the reefer he had a smaller box that he filled with blocks of ice to keep the load cool during the trip. Farmers were also key customers for Art, especially in the spring, when he hauled seed and fertilizer to them for planting. Then at harvest time he was busy hauling grain and potatoes from the farms to market or to warehouses. Some years this demand continued on into late fall and early winter. In late winter he hauled ice from his father's pond to private ice houses and to his own warehouse in the village. The following summer he hauled some of the same ice to the fish plant in Souris.

If he was too busy elsewhere, his brother Leonard would make these trips, driving his new 1952 one ton Ford. Under Art's sponsorship, his younger brother Joe drove an old green 1947 Ford dump truck, hauling gravel and rocks to the new highway bridge at Mount Stewart and other destinations.

Veteran Lornie Smith, Oliver's brother, bought a new, red three ton Studebaker truck that had a hydraulic hoist and dump box installed on it. That summer the Department of Highways was rebuilding the road through Fort Augustus about six miles from the village on the South side of the river. Lornie got a job hauling gravel from a pit at the head of the river to the highway construction site.

Another returned veteran, Bill MacGregor, also purchased a new Studebaker truck with the hoist and dump box factory-installed. He got hired on the same run as Lornie, hauling gravel from the pit to the construction site at Fort Augustus. On Saturdays or summer vacation, when these two truck drivers were making their runs from the pit to the construction site, Donald and I would be waiting at the end of our back lane. They took turns picking us up and taking us with them to Fort Augustus and back. Here again were these two veterans wanting to do everything they could to brighten Donald's day, because Donald had lost his father overseas. I just went along for the ride.

Barney and Me

Past the bridge over the Pisquid river was a long, tough rise called MacKinnon's hill that drivers couldn't get a run at because they had just made a right hand turn at Fred's corner before the bridge. Donald and I would quietly compare Bill and Lornie's driving skills to see how many times they had to gear down going up that hill with a load on. The transmission was usually in 'bull low' by the time they reached the top. Coming back empty, both Lornie and Bill would see how fast they could go, because they were paid by the trip, and Donald and I were urging them on.

Before he had his own truck, Cy 'Duke' MacDonald drove a three ton cab-over Ford for the Co-op sawmill, hauling logs from farms to the mill and lumber from the mill to their customers. His own truck, similar to Art's, was a three ton Dodge, a flat bed with a stake body, and he hauled a lot of the same product as Art. He also hauled fish from the harbours on the North side of the Island to market, processors or cold storage. Later Cy also bought a one ton Dodge for shorter trips and lighter loads.

Like Art Doyle, Romald MacDonald from Maple Hill bought a three ton Ford truck and hauled canned strawberry jam in cartons from the cannery. He also trucked excess strawberries into cold storage in the city, and when they were needed for canning, he would truck them back to the village. Romald was also one of the first truckers in our area to add a trailing axle to the back of his truck, so he could haul bigger loads and lessen the risk of getting charged for being overweight. This axle was mounted so that when the truck was empty the tires and wheels were suspended above the surface of the road, but when the truck was heavily loaded the tires rested on the road and absorbed some of the weight. One problem with this axle was that it had no power, and whether the truck was empty or not, when backing up on difficult terrain, it might get hung up and take the weight off the drive axle, so that its wheels couldn't get enough traction and would spin out. Romald would be stuck and would need a tow.

Every year in the fall, Romald rounded up enough Christmas trees from his brother Clarence, from his own farm, and from other farmers to make a load of several hundred trees to haul to Boston and sell there. That was in late November or early December. For those trips he put extensions on his stake racks and added a custom roof rack over the cab of the truck that was supported in front on two legs resting on the front bumper. There was not a lot of weight in a load of Christmas trees, so all he had to worry about was tying them down securely and staying under the height restrictions on the different highways between home and Boston. Donald and I were friends of Romald's two sons, Grant and Roddy, and we liked to climb, so when we got older, we helped to build the loads of trees for Boston. We secretly wished we could go on a trip to 'the Boston States' but never got an invitation.

The adults would not have wanted the responsibility of two young boys, and our parents may not have endorsed it either.

Chapter 23

Advent of Electricity

Shortly before we moved into the village, Grampy Jay acquired some basic electrical service. Wiring consisted of two uninsulated wires running parallel to each other, with crossbar-like porcelain insulators at intervals to prevent wooden walls and beams from catching fire. An open junction box had a small metal lever that hinged, so you could open or close it to contact another terminal. This was the on/off switch. The initial service was for lights only, and at first it was provided only for two hours in the early evening by a generator that was powered by the water wheel at Laird's mill, three miles away in Pisquid East. This was after the saw mill had been shut down at the end of the day's work. Around the same time, Grampy even had his small barn wired, including one light bulb in the rafters of the loft. The lights in his barn came in handy during the fox skinning season, when customers brought their freshly killed foxes to him in the evening, sometimes after dark, so they would be there for skinning the next morning. In those early days it was an exception and something of a luxury to have your barn wired.

When Daddy decided 'to get the lights in', he contacted the only electrician in the area, Cecil MacAssey from Cherry Hill, where my Mom came from before she married Daddy. Cecil was quiet, polite and kind, a bachelor, who didn't encourage a lot of questions from an inquisitive boy like me. Generally, his message was, "Stand back. Look, but don't touch."

Cecil installed a new type of insulated copper wiring in our house and battled with plaster walls and lathes to get the lights and switches to their destinations. Most of the wall plugs, no more than one in each room, were mounted in the baseboards, which were at least eight inches high and had few or no lathes or plaster behind them. He installed one light in the center of each room's ceiling, upstairs and down. Most of them were equipped with a pull chain and a string extension that had a small metal tag on the end of it, so we could find it in the dark. The lights in the kitchen and dining room, living room and halls were operated from wall switches. The switch plate in the front hall had no less than three switches in it. That was really something.

To wire the ground floor Cecil had to take up floorboards in the bedrooms upstairs. To wire the upstairs, he had to go into the attic. The light in the cellar had a wall switch in the laundry room above the cellar stairs, and the kitchen had two wall plugs, one for the new electric radio, and one for the nearly new electric toaster at the other end.

The toaster was basic, with doors on each side that dropped down like a tail gate on a truck, so you could put bread in and take toast out. You had to stay there and watch it, so the toast didn't burn. There was no thermostat on the toaster. I can't remember which came first, the toaster or sliced bread.

Not all appliances were new, and they were acquired only when the budget would allow, but the most magnificent of all the appliances was this new, big white enamel metal box, called a refrigerator, to keep food cool in summer. It even had a smaller inner box that made ice cubes and could freeze small amounts of meat and fish. When you opened the door, a light came on inside, and it would shut off when you closed the door. We used to play with that light switch when no adults were looking.

Chapter 24

Village Restaurants

The first restaurant in the village, according to Donald, was Mac's Restaurant, operated by Cy 'Duke' MacDonald's mother, Addie, and assisted by her husband Urban 'Bornish' MacDonald. They sold hot dogs, hamburgers, french fries, potato chips and pop. Donald and I never ate there because we were too young. After the war, a returned veteran from New Brunswick, Ray Gallagher, married Cy's sister Helen and gradually took over the restaurant and moved it into a newer building. It had a long counter with a row of stools where customers could sit and eat and a sun porch on the front of the building next to the street that housed a pin-ball machine.

Pin-ball was a first for Donald and me, and it only cost a nickel to play. At first we watched older boys and men and tried to learn the tricks to keep the ball in play. When one ball dropped out of play, two more were activated one at a time by a spring loaded plunger at the business end of the machine. The score for each ball was kept on the scoreboard at the front of the machine, which also showed the score attained by the last player and the highest overall score. The object was to keep each ball in play as long as possible and to beat that high score. There were no prizes, just 'braggin rights'.

About the same time, another veteran from the village, Oliver Smith, came home, married Freida Affleck and opened another restaurant just down the street from Mac's. It was in the front room of their house and sold the same fare as Mac's. It had tables and chairs and a short counter. It was there that I ate my first ever hamburger, which I enjoyed immensely, and it was certainly not my last.

One Saturday evening after dark, early that winter with fresh snow on the ground, I was walking up the sidewalk from MacLeod Douglas' store with someone else, not Donald, when we noticed a commotion outside Smith's restaurant. As we got closer, a crowd gathered, and in the middle of the front lawn two young men were squaring off, fists cocked ready to fight. I recognized the taller boy as one of my many first cousins, Arthur from Pisquid West. His opponent was one of the Kellys from Fort Augustus who had a reputation as a scrapper. With the skiff of snow on the ground, their footing wasn't very good. The crowd was egging them on, and I feared for Arthur because I didn't know if he could fight. There was a quick skirmish between the two, then a flurry of punches, and before you knew it, the Kelly boy was flat on his back, but 'still kickin'. Someone helped Kelly up, he brushed himself off, made a few parting remarks, and the crowd dispersed. That was the first real fight I ever saw, and I was proud of my cousin Art for how he handled himself. I never did hear what the fight was about, maybe something said earlier, because they both attended the same school, or maybe it was over a girl. Sometimes that was the case.

Oliver's restaurant ran for another couple of years, but then Oliver went fishing with his father one spring, and Freida had difficulty running the restaurant alone. There was also competition from Mac's up the street, so they closed down. Mac's continued to operate for a number of years before it too closed and converted to a small market with groceries and meats, which continued as such until it closed in the mid-nineties. It later opened once more as a restaurant under new management, and is still so today, representing at least one building in the village that has gone full circle. Others have not been quite so fortunate.

Chapter 25

Mom's Kitchen

Although our favourite Sunday dinner was Mom's oven-roasted beef with gravy and home-cooked trimmings, the roast and the time and the money were not always available. In that case, on a cold winter Saturday night during our early days in the village, Daddy and I would go to the barn to the quiet chicken roost, choose a hen that had quit laying eggs and take her to the chopping block in the woodshed. I would hold the lantern, and he would hold the sleepy hen by the legs with his left hand, place her neck on the chopping block, and cut her head off with one swipe of the axe. Daddy would drop her on the floor, and we'd step back so that we didn't get splashed with blood. When she stopped kicking and flapping her wings, Daddy would pick her up by a wing or a leg and carry her to the back porch. I'd pick up the head and throw it where the cats could find it outside behind the wood pile.

Meanwhile Mom had boiled a large pot of water on the kitchen stove. Daddy would submerge the hen in the boiling water to loosen the feathers, a process that gave off a distinctly unpleasant smell. Daddy spread newspapers on the porch couch, and when the hen was ready to be plucked, he'd take the cover off the pot and do a test pull on the feathers. If the feathers came out freely, he'd pick the hen out of the pot, dry her off with an old towel, place her on the newspapers, pluck the feathers out a few at a time with his bare hands and drop them into an old bucket. The larger feathers came out easily, but the pin feathers closer to the skin had to be plucked with the blade of his pocket knife against his thumb.

Mom would get the feathers Daddy missed while she was cleaning the insides out of the chicken in the kitchen, saving the heart and the gizzard for gravy. She would roll the insides up in another double layer of newspaper and burn them in the kitchen stove, which created another not so pleasant smell. She'd rinse the carcass in a large pan of cold salted water to make it ready for stuffing on Sunday morning, then she'd cover it and put it in the cool porch overnight.

Sunday morning Mom would bring the chicken into the kitchen, stuff it with the delicious stuffing that she had made from scratch, place it in the roaster and cook it in the oven of the kitchen stove. Some mornings, depending on how she felt, she'd stay home and cook the Sunday dinner. Other Sundays she would put everything on warm and finish cooking dinner when she got home from church. She would always have something homemade for dessert to top off another memorable Mom's Sunday dinner. We'd really be hungry by the time dinner was ready, but it was always worth waiting for.

One spring weekend Daddy brought home a full grown Muscovey duck when he returned from the railway. It looked scrawny and not well fed. He said it had its wings clipped so it wouldn't fly away, and he put it in the woodshed temporarily. Meanwhile, he suggested that I build a pen for it down by Walsh's pond so it would be near the water. I rounded up some old chicken wire about three feet high and four small used fence posts sharpened on one end, and I took them down to the pond.

I built the pen about six feet square, braced the posts with used pieces of 2 x 4, and set it so one corner of it was in the water. Donald helped me when he could. I don't know if Daddy ever got permission from Walsh's for me to do this, but they seemed to approve and saved table scraps for me to feed to the duck. The next weekend when Daddy came home, he went down to the pond to see the duck pen. He was obviously impressed, and with a grin he said, "It sure looks strong enough, but son, you're not going to keep a tiger in here, just a duck." Anyway, he went back to the woodshed and brought the duck down and put it in the pen. The duck looked around briefly and headed straight for the water.

Donald and I fed the duck almost every day with oats, grass, weeds, anything it would eat. He could also eat the vegetation in the floor of the pen. He soon grew bigger and healthier looking. When he got fattened-up, one Saturday evening in the fall, Daddy decided it was time to have a duck dinner. We got the duck from its pen and brought it up to the chopping block in the wood-shed. Like the hen previously, he held the duck by its feet and placed its head and neck on the block. The duck didn't struggle at first, but when Daddy swung the axe, it ducked, and the axe only cut its bill off. It flapped its wings and squawked, but only bled a little bit. Daddy held on to its feet until it settled down, and on the second try he managed to decapitate the duck completely.

The next day Mom cooked a nice Sunday duck dinner. I didn't really enjoy the dinner because while the duck was in the pen I had become attached to it, but I did enjoy dessert.

Like most other housewives of the day, Mom was also an accomplished baker. She baked a batch of biscuits almost every weekday and cookies or a sweet loaf every second day, depending on the state of the larder. My favourites were molasses cookies with raisins in them and sugar cookies with or without raisins. She baked cakes for special occasions and a variety of pies when the ingredients were available. She also baked a loaf she called a 'sultana cake' with mixed fruit in it. Sometimes she baked small shortbread cookies that she called 'scotch cakes', and if she had time, she decorated them with icing and pieces of maraschino cherries.

Another favourite of mine and my sisters were Mom's

cinnamon rolls, which she turned out at least once a month. When I first left home, every now and then I received a small parcel in the mail from home, and I could tell by the shape of it that it was a King Cole tea box with a few of Mom's cinnamon rolls wrapped in wax paper. What a surprise and a treat that I would share with some of my close troop mates who were always hungry like me. Occasionally she even sent cinnamon rolls in the tea box for my wife and I after we got married, and she always made some for me when she knew I was coming home for a visit.

In season, Mom made rhubarb, blueberry, strawberry and plum jams, also green tomato chow, rhubarb relish and mustard pickles, enough to last most of the winter, and I helped her store the full bottles in the cellar. What a glorious aroma greeted me and anyone else who walked into Mom's kitchen on a crisp fall day when she was cooking jams or pickles.

To economize her strength in her middle years, Mom sometimes sat down while she worked, with a pan or bowl in her lap. She had very few bowls. When I moved away and got my first pay cheque, I went to Eaton's and bought a set of four Pyrex mixing bowls and had them sent home to her. She was 'tickled pink' to get them and still had two bowls left when she gave up housekeeping in her later years. She gladly gave them back to me, and we still use them in our cottage.

In the corner of the kitchen next to the firebox end of

the stove was a haven for the weary to rest, the beloved kitchen couch. The frame of the early one was made of steel angle rails and crossbars with slats of fine steel running the length of the couch supported at both ends by short, strong steel springs. The mattress was a hard four inch thick pad that could withstand children jumping on it, but not all that comfortable. There was also a selection of cushions available at the head of the couch next to the outside wall that sometimes became the tools of a pillow fight. This old couch was later moved to the sun porch.

The replacement model, called a studio couch, had a steel frame with an insert in the bottom that slid out to make a bed where children could sleep while they gave up their bed to overnight guests. This couch had an upholstered mattress with three cushions that stood on edge against the wall as a backrest. Together they also served as the mattress for the slide-out bed. This was one cosy place to sleep next to the fire in the kitchen stove on a stormy winter's night. I know, because I did it many times.

The real convenience of the kitchen couch was illustrated when one of us children became sick, especially with a fever, when it became a home infirmary. In the morning when the healthy ones had gone to school, Mom would bring the sick one down to the couch where she could feed the child hot soup and crackers or toast plus whatever home remedy she chose to use. Most of all she could observe, take temperatures and keep blankets on the child to keep him or her comfortable. She managed all of this while she continued her daily chores and perhaps entertained a concerned neighbour who had heard about the ailing child and dropped in to offer help. The visitor might even sit at the foot of the couch because it was right next to the back door and there was no need to remove shoes or boots.

This couch was also where Grammie Jay came one morning, having attempted to continue housekeeping on her own for several years after Grampy died. She threw herself down and declared to my mother, "That's it. I'm tired of trying to keep house alone. Find me a place in a senior's home in town." Mom and Daddy obliged, and Grammie lived to be ninety-seven years old.

Strategically placed between the couch and the stove was a small heirloom rocking chair. In the evenings sometimes, after my two older sisters moved away, I would help Mom by rocking one of my younger sisters to sleep while softly attempting to sing a lullaby.

Chapter 26

Repair Garages in the Village

Like anywhere in North America, the late 1930s and early 1940s were the end of an era of certain styles of cars and trucks, those with square corners, wooden spokes in their wheels, poor quality rubber in their tires, flat windshields, and manual cranks to start engines. Very few people in the village and surrounding areas could afford a new car, and the prevalence of older vehicles was compounded by the World War Two. When we got big enough to turn the crank on a car engine, we were warned never to wrap our thumb around the handle in case the engine kicked back. Steel rims and tires with tubes, manual tire pumps, tire and tube repair kits, four way wrenches, screw jacks with folding crank handles, and water cooled engines were still the norm coming off the assembly lines.

Before the introduction of anti-freeze, farmers had to drain their car radiators and engine blocks every fall and store their cars away for the winter. Some jacked their cars up on blocks to save the tires. Failure to drain the radiator and engine block thoroughly could result in cracks in either one or both when spring came and water was poured into them. Here entered the mechanic, the repairman who might be able to solder the radiator or pour a sealant into the engine block as a temporary measure, but if that didn't work, one or the other might have to be replaced.

Early service and repair garages in the village started out with dirt parking lots and floors, later improved with concrete. In addition to the repairs I just mentioned, the mechanics performed other labour-intensive jobs like tire repairs, using pry bars fashioned from old spring leafs from cars, sledge hammers and screw jacks like those used on the railroad. In the late 1940s and early 1950s came portable hydraulic jacks, and even later came hydraulic hoists that would pick the entire car up and raise it into the air so they could stand under it. Prior to this, each garage had a grease pit in the ground that was the approximate length of a car, roughly three feet wide and deep enough for a short man to work underneath a car or truck. Most grease pits were accessible only by a ladder at one end, which made the pit a death trap if a fire occurred at the end with the ladder and the mechanic in the pit was unable to get out before someone above could move the vehicle off the pit.

When Donald and I were still young, there were only three service and repair garages in the village, all on the business side, the north side of the river. The other repair shop was run by a back yard mechanic, Basil Jay, who worked out of his barn on our side of the river, right next door to us beside the back lane, only two doors from Donald's house. In the late 1940's Basil packed up his family and moved to Newcastle, New Brunswick.

Across the bridge, Danny Clark ran the White Rose service station and garage on the right as we crossed the bridge. It had a concrete floor and a concrete base for the gas tanks. Besides selling gasoline, Danny did repairs and servicing to most cars and trucks, assisted by another mechanic and a helper. This was also a place for the young men to gather with their vehicles and brag about how powerful their engines were and how fast their cars could go. Ultimately, a challenge would be made between two drivers to race each other on the one mile paved stretch of highway a couple of miles east of the village, called 'the MacKenzie straightaway'. They usually took along someone to be a starter and a friend or two to be witnesses. Donald and I were too young to go and never got invited.

Once at the straightaway, the two cars lined up side by side at the east end of the two-lane highway, and the drivers hoped that no oncoming traffic would appear. On the signal from the starter, the two cars would take-off, race as fast as they could to the Cherry Hill road, which was on a right hand curve one mile away. If nothing untoward happened, the race was over in about a minute, and they all returned to the garage. The winner would brag about his great car and his supreme driving skills, while the loser would make excuses, and that would be it until another day.

Danny's garage, on occasion, was also the place for competitive, good natured feats of strength. One man might lift the back end of a small car off the ground or another would lift a heavy object like a rear leaf spring from a big truck over his head or do a one arm push up while picking a wooden match with his teeth from between the fingers of the hand on the floor.

Danny also painted and sponsored a stock car each year to race at the track in Covehead about twenty-five miles away. Ivan Leard, the regular driver, was fearless and won his share of races. Oh, how Donald and I envied him, and we only got to see him race once or twice. One night, after a pile-up, Ivan's car ended up on the roof of another stock car, with his engine still running, the rear wheels still spinning and the sparks flying from the rotating drive shaft.

In the North end of the village, known as 'happy town', Ralph Dunn, he too a War Veteran, operated a small repair garage with no gas pumps. He was the mechanic and had one apprentice helper. His parking lot was not paved, and I'm not sure if his garage floor was either. Donald and I only visited there a couple of times.

At the top of Main Street, on the corner of St. Peters Road, was Danny Mullins' garage, an Irving service station and Chrysler dealership. It was the largest garage in the village by a long shot. He had two full time mechanics and a book keeper, Harold 'Shellduck' MacDonald. Danny took care of car sales himself. His garage had concrete floors throughout, a concrete base and apron at the pumps, and large plate glass windows in the showroom. He was also the designer and builder of a rear propeller-driven snow mobile on skis and the owner of the first Bombardier snow mobile on tracks and front skis in the area.

As an aside, my father bought new 1950, 1953, 1955, 1958 and 1960 Plymouth cars from him. As my eldest sister would say, "Daddy sure loved his cars." I got my Driver's License with the '53, but my favourite was the '55, which was a bigger car with a bigger engine, and it could fly!

Eileen, Connie, and me in front of our 1933 Frontenac

Barney and Me with my sisters, Miriam and Cynthia

Chapter 27

Welcome Bathtub and Indoor Toilet

Two or three years after we moved to the village, my father cut a large hole in the front of the house roof directly above the front door and installed a dormer, creating a space big enough for our new bathroom. He hired Ben Birt, the plumber, to install the fixtures in the bathroom, kitchen and laundry room, and a hot water tank behind the kitchen stove. Ben was a large jovial man who had no children and simply fascinated me. Whenever I was around he used me as a gopher and helper, a task I gratefully accepted.

The hot and cold water lines were half-inch steel pipe that had to be cut, threaded and fitted with elbows and couplings to connect a tank at one end and a tap at the other. All pipes had to be routed through the house, some hidden and some outside the walls where Daddy boxed them in later. The bathtub, second-hand from the city, had 'tiger-paw' ornamental legs and a combined hot and cold water tap. The bathroom sink was long and narrow on the opposite wall from the tub. It had two separate taps, as did the kitchen sink and the laundry tub. Drain pipes from all units were galvanized steel, like the water pipes, only much larger in diameter. All had to be cut and threaded, fitted and connected together.

To thread each pipe at both ends, Ben used a manually operated threader, mounted on a tripod that was as tall as I was, made of three heavy-gauge steel pipes as legs and powered by a long steel bar with Ben on the end of it. Each time he threaded a different size pipe, he changed the teeth in the threader. Before and sometimes during the threading he squirted oil onto the part of the pipe to be threaded, to make it easier for the teeth to cut into the metal and the bar easier to turn.

The main drain pipe from the bathroom fixtures, including the toilet, ran down into the cellar and ultimately outside, going downhill all the way to the river. It was four inch diameter cast iron pipe that was connected by soldering the joints. To do that, Ben had a blow torch for heat and a long handled ladle to melt the solder and pour it into the joint to be sealed. In the bathroom, he had to rip up the floor boards to install this pipe and connect it to the toilet, then run it down through the first floor into the cellar. When he finished, he put the floor back together, and Daddy later boxed in the pipes between the first and second floor.

Outside at the back of the house, Daddy and a helper dug a short trench by hand, three to four feet deep to stay below the frost, from Grampy's well into our cellar where the big galvanized cold water tank and electric pump were located. The sewer line emerged from the cellar where the cold water line went in and another longer trench was dug through our back yard and the neighbour's yard, owned by my grandfather, all the way down to the river. At that time, anyone with indoor plumbing did the same thing, dumped raw sewage into the river. That was corrected years later by the arrival of a sewage treatment plant.

Chapter 28

Toilet Paper and Kleenex

Before indoor plumbing arrived in the rural part of our little Island, the outdoor toilet, 'the privey' or 'the little brown building', was the go-to place when nature called. Outdoor toilets came in all shapes and sizes, new and nearly new to run down and dilapidated. They were located anywhere from a lonely corner of a small field near the house, to the backyard fifty yards from the house, to a discreet spot tucked away inside the barn, to an outbuilding, painted the same color to blend in.

Some had a window pane in the door and some had a window on the side, both high enough off the ground, so that kids couldn't peek in. Some had no window at all. If you wanted light you had to leave the door ajar in the daytime or bring a lantern after dark. Most had one hole, but grandfather's and Uncle Harold's had two, so if two girls or two boys had to go at the same time, they could and also have a little chat. Most toilets had a loose piece of oval-shaped board to cover the holes.

My sister-in-law and her boyfriend, when they were

teenagers, used to visit family friends, a couple with no children, after dark. Before they went into the house, as a prank, they went to the outdoor toilet and dropped the cover down the hole. Then they would visit, have tea and cookies, snicker and laugh during the visit, and laugh all the way home imagining the reaction of their hosts when they went to the toilet the next morning.

All toilets had a very necessary feature, a hatch at the back or the side, so that the accumulated contents could be cleaned out once a year, usually in the spring. It could then be added to the manure or the 'top dress' and cultivated into the garden or field. Now that was one chore that the men and older boys of the household avoided whenever possible.

Another basic necessity in any toilet was, and still is, something disposable with which to wipe one's behind. Before Donald's and my time poor people are said to have used pages from the Eaton's catalogue because it was free, but it sure must have lacked in comfort and effectiveness. Our parents and grandparents could afford a daily newspaper, considerably better than T. Eaton's donation, and that was what we used as children. When toilet paper arrived, total bliss, but it was tempered with restrictions on how many sheets we could use in one sitting.

Toilet paper also replaced handkerchiefs in the house when anyone had a cold. Then, after the World War Two, circa 1946-47, came Kleenex! I remember vividly the first box that came into our house. It was about the same size as those still in the dispensers of hotels and motels. Most intriguing were the two perforated flaps at one edge of the bottom of the box that could be partially cut out, hinged away from the box, and pinned to the wall with two thumb tacks. I was honored to be the one to complete that first installation on our kitchen wall by the back door. Once again, use was restricted to a need only basis, and we were encouraged to get more than one blow out of each tissue. When all usable space was exhausted on the tissue, it was to be immediately thrown into the kitchen stove, whether lighted or not. That way, we hoped to limit the spread of germs and also contribute to lighting the fire the next morning.

In rural P.E.I., on cold wintry days before the arrival of Kleenex, a drip from a child's nose might be snuffed back and swallowed, licked from the upper lip, or casually wiped on a nearby sleeve. Adult males working outdoors did the same, except instead of swallowing, they spit it out onto the snow and stepped on it. The adult male working outdoors or in the barn, who had a head cold and was without a hankie or Kleenex, might be obliged to press a finger against one nostril, turn his back to the wind, and exhale vigorously. This maneuver was a no-no in the presence of ladies. Donald and I grew up in the presence of these habits, and even today, if circumstances permit, I still cough it up and spit it out, much to my wife's chagrin.

Chapter 29

Pal

In the late 1940s, Donald was given a newly weaned puppy by my uncle Clarence. He was just a mongrel, brown to tan in color with no markings, perhaps a cross between a Newfoundland and a Labrador retriever. Donald was eight or nine years of age at the time and named the puppy Pal. From that time forward, Donald and Pal were almost inseparable and, as time passed, I was included in most of their adventures. We taught Pal how to come when we called and a few everyday commands, but the one that was the most fun was "sic–um", which was a common command among dog owners of the day when they wanted their dog to chase something or someone. We never taught Pal to chase people, but he sure liked to chase cats, though he rarely ever caught one.

As Pal grew bigger and stronger and winter came, he became more difficult to control, because if we held his collar he could easily drag one of us through the snow. Two of us could hold him if we had to. Then one day we had a hand sleigh with us, and we tied a rope to Pal's collar. He could pull the sleigh with one of us on it a short distance, but the ride was kind of erratic because he would grab the rope in his teeth and turn around and get all tangled up in it. So one day, our neighbor Freeman saw our predicament and gave Donald a dog harness that was basically a padded leather collar with two leather traces attached. The collar didn't open, but it was big enough to pull on over Pal's head, and we hooked the traces to the sleigh with pieces of binder twine. One of us would get on the sleigh. The other would lead Pal by the collar to get him started and then jump on too. If another dog or a cat or a car went by, Pal would take off after it, and we'd have a merry ride until Pal turned or tried to stop. The sleigh would either go straight or take the feet out from under him. What a laugh we'd have when that happened, because we'd roll off the sleigh and hug Pal and try to apologize to him for being so mean.

When my father, who was usually only home on the weekends, heard about this, he offered to build a set of hardwood shafts for the sleigh as well as fashion a back-pad and a girth strap from old horse harness so that the shafts could be fastened to Pal's body. The rest of the winter we had some great trips with Pal and the sleigh when the weather and the roads and the river ice permitted. Pal really loved to chase after a horse and sleigh on the river ice. We would have to watch that we didn't get too close, or we might get a scolding from the driver, or worse, get a tap on the head from a sleigh stake. We could easily stop Pal if we both rolled off and held onto the sleigh and dragged behind it in the snow.

At full size, Pal weighed eighty or ninety pounds. As he grew, he had the best of food (no canned dog food in those days), including table scraps from home and from neighbours who didn't have a dog, as well as scraps of meat and bones from Affleck's meat market and slaughter house, where he went himself anytime he was hungry for a treat. If Pal got a large bone, say part of a cow's leg, he would carry it home in his mouth to enjoy in his back yard, and what he didn't eat he buried in the snow or the ground.

Pal had a mind of his own, and if he felt like going for a visit, he went. He had a reputation of being a big dog that anyone could pet, even a child. In Donald's words, "He wouldn't hurt a flea." Donald's mother Rita always said that Pal was the cleanest dog she ever knew. In summer, if he felt like going for a swim in the river, he went. In winter, he simply rolled in the snow, then got up and shook himself.

Winter and summer, everywhere Donald and I went, Pal followed or ran ahead. There were no leashes or stoop-and-scoop bags for dog owners. People just had to be careful where they stepped. All in all we had some glorious times together, Pal, Donald and I.

Then one day when Pal was about five years old, Donald and Pal were playing in the vacant schoolyard. One of the village kids, a boy younger than Donald, stopped by.

He had a plastic pirate's knife, and he playfully threatened Donald with it. Pal took the threat as real, bit the boy in the leg, and the boy ran home crying. The next day Pal was on the street with Donald's cousin Ramona. The boy's father came by in his car and persuaded Ramona to lure Pal into the car. He drove a short distance and let Ramona out, then he took Pal to Cart Point, an isolated wharf by the river south of the village, and shot him. Donald didn't find out until days later when someone discovered the dog's body lying beside the road to the wharf. Both Donald and I were heartbroken at the news. We knew we'd never see Pal again.

Chapter 30

Our Buddy Reggie

When World War Two ended, Reggie Walsh, another veteran, came home to live with his two spinster sisters in the big house on the far side of Grampy Jay's property. One of the first things he did after he got settled was to buy a big black horse named Tom. He also acquired a truck wagon for Tom to pull in spring, summer and fall, and a wood sleigh for winter. In the summer, Tom pastured in the field in front of our house, when he was not working. He was a kind animal, and all the children on the block used to feed him handfuls of grass and soon became attached to him. Donald and I were no exception.

Tom may have had a lazy streak in him, because in the mornings when Reggie drove him out the back lane to go to his hobby farm up in Cherry Hill, Tom could hardly drag one foot after the other. Then in the evening coming home he looked like a prancing Arabian stallion as he came in the back lane past our house. Through Tom, Donald and I gradually got to know Reggie, who like all the other veterans gave extra time and affection to

Donald, because his father had paid with his life overseas while they had made it back home safely. I just went along for the ride, literally. When we'd see Reggie coming home in the evenings, we'd run out the lane to meet him, jump on the wagon or sleigh, and ride the short distance to the barn. When we got old enough, we'd help to unhitch Tom and put him in the barn and give him some hay.

Reggie was kind, good natured and happy-go-lucky. If he had time, we'd sit in the stable and discuss the events of the day while Tom munched his supper. To me, there is no more peaceful sound than a horse eating his feed in the quiet of a stable, and I'm sure Donald and Reggie felt the same. Reggie sometimes liked to stop and have a drink with a friend on his way home, and on those days he'd be late and more inclined to talk about the war. He had lots of stories to tell, and Donald and I were all ears. Reggie was born circa 1897. His father was a family doctor who lived and practiced from his home, right there in the village. Until cars arrived, his main means of transportation was horses, stabled in that very barn we were sitting in.

According to his sister Evelyn, when Reggie and his brothers were small, they had all the toys they wanted, and when they became old enough, their father bought them air rifles. They roamed the woods outside the village and soon became excellent marksmen. In 1914, when World War One broke out, Reggie signed up for the

Army. He wasn't in the service very long when the officers realized what a crack shot he was and assigned him to the Sniper Corps overseas. One sunny day in France, Reggie was standing guard over a group of soldiers rebuilding a damaged bridge when he caught a glimpse of something shiny high up in a large tree across the river. He took aim at the flash and pulled the trigger. An enemy sniper tumbled out of the tree like a wounded goose. Reggie would smile with pride and satisfaction as he related this story.

Unlike some veterans, Reggie was not a braggart, but was very modest about his adventures. He admitted the only time he was wounded was one night when he and his buddies were climbing up onto the back of an army truck to go back to camp and he fell backwards onto the bayonet of the soldier behind him. By the time the wound was discovered and attended to days later, infection had set in, and he lost part of one lung and some ribs. He never showed us the wound. When we asked, "Did that hurt?" he replied, with a twinkle in his eye, that they were coming back from a night on the town when it happened, and that he was "feelin no pain".

When we were young, the Mount Stewart Post Office was the distribution centre for all the outlying communities within a twenty-five mile radius of the village. Every weekday evening, the train would drop the mail at the railway station, which was in itself a hub for that part of the Island. Every morning, Monday through Saturday, the mail drivers for each district gathered in the room at the back of the Post Office to sort and package their mail for the day. This was also an arena in which to tell stories and poke fun at each other. Some drivers had cars to drive their routes, and others still drove horses, summer and winter. Even those with cars, like my uncle Clarence, drove horses in the late winter and early spring, when the frost came out of the ground and the dirt roads were impassable by car. The only paved roads were the main street in the village and the portion of St. Peter's highway that passed north of the village. Some of the horses on the mail routes were not the most attractive, but they were rugged and durable.

In those days when a horse got old or broken down and no longer able to do a day's work it was usually put out of its misery by shooting it. If it had been a long-serving, faithful horse to the owner, a large hole was dug by hand in a field near the barn, and the horse, almost ceremoniously, was laid to rest. If the meat was deemed fit for animal consumption and the owner needed the money, it would be butchered and sold to feed the tame foxes. If the owner didn't care, he might hook another horse onto it, drag it back to the woods, and let the wild animals, crows and ravens pick away until there was nothing left but the bones. The latter method was the origin of one horse owner poking fun at another man's horse, regardless of its condition, by calling it crow's bait.

Two of the mail drivers were brothers from the village,

and one seemed to be continuously trading horses, trying to upgrade his stock. Some of them might be limping or have their ribs showing. This trader became a target for other drivers, who teased him about his horses and told him they looked so poor they should be fed to the crows. Reggie carried this a bit farther by cawing like a crow every time this particular driver went by. The driver would retaliate by cawing back at Reggie, who would just laugh and carry on, until the next encounter. This good-natured banter went on for years between these two. The culmination of all this was that the mail driver inherited the nickname 'Crow', which stuck with him for the rest of his days. As a matter of fact, some of his children inherited that nickname to distinguish them from their cousins with the same last name.

On Saturdays or on X-mas or Easter vacation, Donald and I went with Reggie and Tom out to his farm and helped by piling brush or doing similar jobs. In winter, Reggie set rabbit snares in the woods, and he showed us what rabbit tracks looked like in the snow and how to read their direction of travel. He also showed us the best places to set a snare and how to make one out of rabbit wire. One day, when Donald and I were with him checking the trap line, we found a live rabbit in a snare. Reggie grabbed the rabbit by the hind legs, took the snare from around its neck, swung it and struck its head against a tree to kill it. When he did, the rabbit cried like a baby. I don't remember this, but Donald told me later that when he heard that rabbit cry he almost threw up.

When World War Two had started, Reggie signed up again and was sent to be a guard at a Prisoner of War camp in Northern Ontario, where he remained for the rest of the war. Donald recalls that Reggie also served some time overseas. The main thing is that he returned home, and Donald and I were the benefactors. For instance, when I became old enough to go duck hunting, my Dad didn't have a gun. Reggie taught me how to safely handle, load and shoot his Remington 12-gauge pump-action shotgun. This was not easy, because I was right handed, but couldn't close my left eye. No problem, Reggie taught me how to shoot off my left shoulder, and I've done that all my life. The action on that old shotgun was so worn you could pump it with one finger and a thumb, but it was true, and it could hit, if you gave it a chance.

Meanwhile, Donald was experimenting with his uncle's double-barreled 10 gauge shotgun, but it was too heavy, and kicked like a mule. Donald then borrowed Mugridge's long barrel 12-gauge shotgun, affectionately called 'Long Tom', so we were all set.

Reggie had shown me where his gun and ammunition were kept in the barn and had told me I could borrow it anytime, as long as I had my parent's approval. So when hunting season opened that fall, the first Saturday, Donald and I headed up along the marsh to the head of the river to hunt black ducks and green-winged teal. We fired at a couple of ducks on the wing, but didn't hit any, and I fell into a muskrat hole along the river bank, getting soaked to the waist. Scott Walker came along and helped me out.

Later that season, I went duck hunting with my cousin Garth and our uncle Willard to the marsh at the head of the river one evening just before dusk. Before our uncle arrived from town, Garth and I had some time to kill, so we took the guns and an old fertilizer bag as a target to the field behind the barn to practice. As we walked across the barn yard, Garth was walking ahead of me. I was impatient and opened the breach of Reggie's old pump gun, inserted a shell and racked the action ahead. When I did, the gun went off and turned up the sod about six feet behind Garth's foot. Thank God that Reggie had taught me always to keep the muzzle of the gun pointed at the ground. That was the end of the target practice, because we both were too shaken to shoot anything.

Later, down at the river, a lone green-winged teal flew past. I shot it with Reggie's gun, and it fell onto the marsh, where I was able to retrieve it without a dog. I was as proud as a peacock with my first kill and retrieval of a very small duck. I gave it to Aunt Alice to clean and cook.

Reggie was alive and well when I left home as a teen, and I always visited with him when I came back home on vacation. He was an active member of the local Legion, which was started up by him and other local veterans. He was a good friend to a couple of adventurous boys, and we will always remember him.

Chapter 31

War Stories

On warm spring days when Donald and I were between seven and ten years old, Grampy Jay and Donald's grand-uncle, Danny 'Jimmy' MacDonald could be found sitting in the sun on a pile of lumber on the South side of Grampy's workshop. At this stage of their lives, they were both close in age and retired, with time on their hands. Their real life stories, however, were as different as night and day. Danny was a confirmed bachelor who, except for his military service in World War One, had lived most of his life at home with one of his sisters on the other side of Donald's house. He was now at home in the village living off his pension. Both men were very competitive, and eventually their life experiences in their younger days would take on the flair of entertainment, with one trying to outdo the other. When Donald and I would drop by and sit down beside them, it was obvious even to our innocent ears that the competition led to exaggeration which soon became the rule rather than the exception. Topics included the hungry thirties and the drastic measures each had to take in order for them and their families to survive. There were stories of heroics by each of them in the most precarious circumstances, like falling through the river ice in the springtime and how, alone or with the help of passers-by, they rescued themselves and their horses.

One of Danny's favorite stories was when he was in the army oversees. One cold and rainy night he and some of his buddies were out on the town drinking. On his way back to camp Danny got separated from his unit and got lost. He came upon a large tent, a make-shift morgue that was partly filled with bodies of fallen soldiers lying in rows on the ground, each one covered with a blanket. Danny crawled into the tent in the darkness and borrowed a blanket from each of two corpses saying, "Sorry old chaps, but I need this more than you do." He lay down beside the corpses and went to sleep. At daybreak, two other soldiers came into the tent carrying another body on a stretcher. Danny woke up, realized it was daylight, and that he might be AWOL. He abruptly sat up and said, "Hey Mac, what time is it?" The two soldiers dropped the stretcher, turned and ran.

Grampy, on the other hand, was the eldest of thirteen children, had never been in the army, and was rarely off the Island where we all lived. His favourite annual trip was in the early fall when he packed his fiddle and a change of clothes, and he and Grammie went in his 1938 Chevrolet coupe across the Northumberland Strait

142

to Antigonish, Nova Scotia. There he visited other old time fiddlers, compared notes and had a few tunes together. He had learned early the responsibility of succeeding his father and taking over the running of the family farm, which he ultimately inherited. He also had learned to play the fiddle and played for his first dance for money at the age of fourteen. I don't know if he ever took a drink of alcohol in his life.

As an adult, besides farming and raising a family, he used to drive taxi, winter and summer, for salesmen who came by train to the village and needed to go to rural communities away from the rail line. Before cars, he drove a horse with no name, simply known as 'The Black Horse'. He would pick up the fare at the station in Mount Stewart or Pisquid and drive him to his destination and back again in time to meet the next train. If an overnight stay was necessary, my grandmother would provide bed and breakfast. The Black Horse had the reputation of never tiring and rarely walking during a trip.

My grandfather was also an accomplished carpenter and built several houses that are still standing. The one I was born in was built by him. It was burned one Halloween night, many years later, after it was abandoned by the family who bought it from Daddy.

Grampy also did early highway construction, standing on the back of a road grader that was pulled by a caterpillar-style tractor driven by another worker. When the operator failed to meet Grampy's expectations, he was replaced by a network of wires and ropes, so Grampy could control the tractor remotely from the back of the grader.

One of Grampy's favourite stories was when he was a young man on the farm. One early spring morning he noticed a calf was missing. There was snow on the ground, and he could see evidence of a struggle and tracks leading away to the woods. He recognized them as bear tracks and followed them into the woods. The tracks led right into a den under a large brush pile. He went back to the farm and called for help. One of the men brought an axe and cut down a small hardwood tree. He cut off the top and the branches and blazed the butt end so that there were sharp jagged shards of wood facing upward but still attached. The men walked back to the den and proceeded to poke the shard end of the pole into the den, making the bear growl and bite at it. Finally the bear grabbed on, and the shards of wood got caught in his teeth. All the men except one grabbed onto the pole and pulled the bear partly out of the den. The lone man then moved in and killed the bear with the axe!

On a lighter topic of hard times, Grampy had another favourite story about how he, being the eldest boy, had to go to the pasture in early morning on his bare feet to get the cows for milking. In the spring and fall the ground was cold and damp, and the cows would be lying down. He'd go to the first cow and kick her to get her up, then stand on the ground where she had been, to warm his feet. He'd repeat this until all the cows were up and then drive them home to the barn for milking.

And so it went, when Danny would tell a story, even before he finished, Grampy would butt in with a bigger and better tale. Donald and I would listen for a while, then one of us, usually Donald, would make a comment like, "Really, is that a fact?" or "Are you sure that's the way it went?" Danny would fake a swat at us and say, "Get outta here before I grab ye by the scruff of the neck and tan yer hide." We'd jump up, run a short distance, and come right back. This time we'd stand near them and taunt them, and they'd gesture us away again. Eventually they'd run out of stories for that day and meet again on another sunny day in the same place.

In summer, the same two gentlemen could be found on Grampy's front lawn, overlooking the river, sitting in folding chairs made by Grampy, with finished, painted red wooden frames and canvas from damaged mail bags that he had retrieved from the railway or the post office. When Donald and I arrived, there were two smaller, similar chairs for us. Most days the same scenario would unfold as in those sunny days of spring outside Gampy's workshop.

One final story from Grampy involved him playing the fiddle alone for a dance at age fifteen in a community five or six miles from home in the community of Fort Augustus. At midnight, when his agreed time was up, he started to pack up his fiddle and go home. One boisterous, ginned-up man accosted him and told him, "You'll leave when we tell you, or we'll send your bones home in the box." Grampy was not a small teenager, and he stood his ground. Soon some cooler heads prevailed and offered to pay him double if he stayed and played until 1:00 A.M. Grampy agreed and walked home alone. I can't remember what double was, maybe another dollar.

What wonderful, fond memories Donald and I have of these two grand, old gentlemen. How precious and convenient one of today's many recording devices would have been. We don't even have a photograph of them together, let alone a sound track or a movie. It would be priceless.

Grampy with his fiddle

Chapter 32

Mills of the Village

After the war, my cousin 'Junior' Coffin, a returned veteran, bought a farm across the Pisquid River from his father, got married, and bought a horse and wood sleigh. He cut logs in his woods and hauled them through the village and across the bridge to the Co-op sawmill. His horse was dark brown, and he looked different from other horses of the day because Junior had cut his black mane in a brush cut.

Donald and I would see Junior coming in the Peakes Road and would run out to meet him, then run beside him all the way across the bridge to the mill. Even Junior would have to get off and run over the bare spots like the concrete center span on the bridge, to lighten the load. On dry days, the sparks would fly from the steel sleigh runners, and the horse would almost get down on his knees to pull the load to the next patch of snow. When we got to the mill, we would help Junior roll the logs off the sleigh so that we could get a ride back across the bridge with him and jump off near home. Some days

Junior would make more than one trip, and we'd be there to help him again. This might be our only excitement in an otherwise boring winter Saturday.

The Co-op mill was located behind the Co-op store on Main Street, just beyond some of the many railway tracks that made up the Mount Stewart Junction. All traffic to and from the mill had to cross at least one set of tracks, and Junior had to cross two. Like the center span of the bridge, the crossings were usually bare and presented a challenge to any horse pulling a load. Some horses from the country that were not used to trains, especially steam engines, would spook as they approached the crossing. The horse might balk and refuse to go, even after the train had passed. He might even try to back up or might jump and turn and go back the way he came 'at a bending gallop'. The latter would be difficult if the wagon or sleigh was fully loaded, but there was always the danger that he would smash something or hurt somebody. Donald and I never really saw this happen, but we heard about it.

We also used to visit Crane's sawmill and were fascinated by the small pond that Mr. Crane used to dunk the logs in to wash them off and make them easier to saw. He had a winch and a steel cable to snare the logs and pull them in, one at a time, lining them up so he could roll them onto the carriage that carried them into the saw. That mill was powered by a big yellow CAT diesel engine, the first one we ever saw. It looked as big as a house to us and really sounded powerful. Mr. Crane's younger brother was his helper at the mill, but when he wasn't there, and we were 'just hangin around', Mr. Crane would ask us to help move or pile some slabs of wood or some smaller pieces of lumber. He wouldn't let us go near any moving equipment like the big saw or drive belts and pulleys. He'd tell us just to stand back and watch.

Mr. Crane also had a shingle mill beside his house, which was up behind the saw mill. It was powered by an old car engine and made wooden shingles for walls and roofs of houses, barns and out buildings. When Crane's son grew old enough, perhaps eleven or twelve, he used to mill shingles by himself. When I was there, I would help him. He would operate the saw to cut the shingles and edge them so they would later fit together, then toss them to me. I would pack them into a pre-jigged box where they could be bundled for sale. When the box was full, one of us would pull the bar down to compress the bundle while the other one nailed the straps to one end of the top cross bar to hold the bundle together. I don't think Donald was ever there with me, and I wasn't there that often myself.

The saw mills and the shingle mill were not only a source of finished products. A by-product from all three was sawdust used to separate and pack blocks of ice, so they would stay cold and not stick together in ice houses. It was also used as bedding for animals and as banking for houses to keep out the winter drafts. Very few homes in the village had concrete basements. They sat on blocks of stone with no mortar between them and had little more than an earth root cellar underneath. So, every fall banking the house was a necessary chore. The saw mills also turned out loads of slabs cut into stove lengths, which were excellent for quick fires in the kitchen stove in spring, summer and fall, and to help start the fire in all stoves in the winter.

The double tenement that our family lived in had no less than four wood or coal burning stoves, two on each side. Mom's mother lived on one side and our family in the other, with a connecting door between. In my early teens, I slept in the spare bed on my grand-mother's side to keep her company at night. On cold winter mornings, because I was the only boy and my father was away on the train, my job was to light all four fires and keep them going until someone else got up and took over from me. Each evening in winter my task was to fetch the wood, coal, and kindling, which I sometimes cut by lantern light. I would bring it to the house from the sheds, all ready for the next morning. The tasks were simple enough, but all too often Donald and I would goof off until after dark, when one of our mothers would call out to remind us to do our chores and then come in to do our lessons for school the next day. It might be dark and cold and almost always windy, so that drifting snow would blow into the woodshed causing the shed door to slam with such force that it would blow out the lantern. Then I would have to go to the house, re-light the lantern

and start all over again. Certainly not the formula for
$^+$A plus marks in school, but we survived.

The fourth mill in the village was the Feed Mill, which
up until recently was still operated by its third owner.
That mill was first opened after World War Two by Fred
Clark, a returned veteran. It was housed in an old Odd
Fellows hall near a railway siding just south of the train
station and backed onto the parking lot of the United
Church. A few years later, in 1952, it was lost to fire
one cold, windy evening. Donald and I were there and
marveled at the flames and confusion as the fledgling fire
department and volunteers tried in vain to fight the fire.
They soon realized that saving the mill was impossible
and concentrated on hosing down the roof of the church
manse which was in the direct line of the wind-blown
sparks and pieces of burning shingles from the fire. The
mill was a total loss.

When it was rebuilt in 1956 on the same site, it too
was a two-storey structure and was powered by a giant
stationery diesel engine. The two floors allowed work
space on both levels and the gravity-fed hoppers on the
second floor offered the convenience of re-directing or
bagging product on the first floor.

The mill operator cleaned grains for local farmers for
seed; mixed grains grown locally with bought concen-
trates for animal feed; sold pre-mixed and pre-bagged
animal feed from wholesalers like Shur-Gain; sold lina-
ments, medication for animals, salt licks, fly spray, lime

and fertilizer and other farmer's needs. The miller would also purchase surplus farm products with cash or with bartered services. Not all farmers paid the mill operator promptly for product or services. Some paid part of their bill at harvest time, and some, a very small percentage, never paid at all. Donald and I only visited the feed mill occasionally, partly because it was across the bridge and partly because we were rarely allowed past the front door for fear we might get in the way, or worse still, get hurt.

My cousin Art was the last full time owner of the mill. He tells me that he went to work for Clark around 1956 and took over the mill in 1963. He operated six days a week and served farmers within a thirty mile area. His motto was, "As long as I am home, the mill is open." In other words, if a customer called and needed something at the mill and Art was home, he'd jump in his car and drive about three city blocks to the mill and open it. Art recalls he ran the mill for thirty-four days straight one spring, cleaning grain for planting, and he's still going strong at eighty years of age.

Chapter 33

Sports and Recreation

Children of today or of generations since the 1940s cannot begin to imagine a world with no organized sports, as was the case in the village of Mount Stewart and the neighbouring villages when we were growing up. Canadian football and soccer were unheard of. The first basketball I saw was in the gym at Prince of Wales College in Charlottetown. The first World Series baseball game I saw was on a neighbour's black and white TV when I was nineteen, and the first CFL game I saw was on my own TV on a Saturday afternoon in the early 1960s when my wife was working and I was waiting to go to work. But I still learned to play hockey, sort of, and continued to play until I was sixty-four.

At college in Grade Eleven, I tried out for the rugby team and played in the first game of rugby I ever saw. At home, a baseball game consisted of a sponge rubber ball of poor quality, no gloves, and a piece of wood representing a bat, which might be a slab of firewood or a small board or a piece of a broken shovel handle. Pieces of wood or stone marked the bases. Both girls and boys played, and the bigger ones made and enforced the rules. We usually played in the parking lot in front of our house with part of Reggie's field as the outfield.

Sometimes the girls would ask the boys to jump skipping rope, and at the risk of being called sissies we might accept, providing we swung the rope for them the required number of times beforehand. For want of something better to, Donald and I would occasionally concede and participate. We even learned some of the chants like: "Peel a banana upside down, peel an orange all around. If you skip to twenty-four, you may have your turn once more." A similar chant was, "Teddy bear, teddy bear, go up stairs, teddy bear, teddy bear, say your prayers. Teddy bear, teddy bear, turn around, teddy bear, teddy bear, touch the ground." Another little ditty went like this: "Mairzy doats and dozy doats and liddle lamzy divey, a kiddily divey too, wouldn't you." Even though we sang it, we didn't know until years later it actually was, "Mares eat oats and does (female deer) eat oats and little lambs eat ivy, a kid (baby goat) will eat ivy too, wouldn't you?"

There was also no shortage of old car tires that we could roll ahead of us as we ran, using our bare hands or two pieces of kindling to keep the tire from falling over. It was even more fun if we rolled the tire through a mud puddle and ran after it.

In winter, almost every family on the block had ac-

cess to a hand sleigh, most homemade of wood, a minia-
ture version of the horse drawn wood sleigh, complete
with steel runners with holes in front to attach a rope
for pulling. My grandfather made ours, and he even included holes in the ends of the bunks so we could put
stakes on the side to keep a load from falling off. I used
it to haul firewood from the woodshed to the house and
pots or buckets of water from the pump to the barn or
house, to take groceries home from the store or small
pieces of freight from the Railway Station to home or to
the neighbours. Sometimes it was all I had to go coasting
with Donald, but it was slow, heavy to pull back up the
hill, and impossible to steer. Donald had a smaller belly
sleigh that was more maneuverable.

One Christmas, my sisters and I were thrilled to find a
new sleigh under the tree. It was not anyone's exclusively,
but would have to be shared with our siblings. Sleds at
the time might be a simple little sleigh or a bigger one
with red steel runners and frame, a 'Flyer' that could
be steered by a wooden handle bar at the front. All of
the wood in new sleighs was varnished with the name
painted in the center board. This was the Cadillac of
coasting sleighs, especially after a January thaw followed
by an overnight freeze which left part or all of a hill like
a bobsled run.

I had one of these sleighs and was on it one day on
MacEachern's hill with Donald coasting beside me, when
I overshot the usual stopping point at the bottom, went

under a three-strand barbed wire fence and tore a strip down the back of my nearly new prized parka. It was silver grey in color, had a fur trimmed hood and a green reflective arm band for walking on the street at night. When we got stopped at the bottom and stood up, Donald said, "You just got a rip down the back of your jacket on that barbed wire." I took the parka off and examined the damage, and we discussed what I could do. With trepidation, I went home and told my mother what happened. She was disappointed, happy I wasn't hurt, understood, and found the time to sew it up so the tear was hardly visible.

When we got older, Donald and I would walk a mile out the Peakes Road or the railway tracks to Romald's, whose sons, Grant and Roddy, were friends of ours, and we'd go coasting with them down Maple Hill in a field on their farm below the road. The hill was steep, and we would get tired walking back up. So one afternoon, Grant said, "Let's take the sides off our box sleigh, raise the shafts up in the air and tie them back to the rear of the sleigh so they won't fall going down the hill. Then we can all climb onto the deck together and enjoy the ride down the hill." But the fun ended at the bottom when we had to turn the big sleigh around and pull or push it back up the hill. So Grant decided after a couple of trips to go to the barn, harness one of the horses, and ride it bareback down the hill ahead of us. Then he would be there to greet us when we coasted down the next time, hitch the horse to the sleigh, and pull it back up the hill with all of us on it. Now that's what you could call luxury coasting. It was the only time we did it, but unforgettable.

Chapter 34

The Movie Theatre

After the war, two MacDonald brothers, Collie and Reggie, both returned veterans, came home to the village and started a movie theatre in the old Memorial Hall down by the river. These were the first movies seen in the village, shows like *The Three Stooges*, *The Great Dan Patch*, *Ma and Pa Kettle, Dean Martin and Jerry Lewis, Dick Tracy* and *Murder Mysteries*. All movies began with cartoons like Bugs Bunny and Elmer Fudd in *Merrie Melodies*. They also showed news serials before the movie started. All were in black and white, and we were excited to go and see them for twenty cents. Movie nights were Friday and Saturday, no matinees.

After two years or so, circa 1947, one night during a movie a fire started in the projection room. Donald and I were too young to be there. The volunteer fire department was called. Two firemen pulled the two-wheeled cart with an old Ford engine, a pump and a length of hose down to the river beside the burning hall and got set up, but they were no match for the inferno in the old wooden hall. Everyone escaped safely without injury, but the hall was lost.

A year or two later, Collie and Reggie built a new theatre in Happy Town, which was the local nickname for the North end of the village. Like the old hall, the floor in the new theatre was flat, not sloped, so the screen had to be elevated above the stage. The projector was in the balcony at the back of the hall. The seats were sections of plain hardwood kitchen chairs bolted to a long wooden plank that held them together. It was said this was so they would be more difficult to tip over or be thrown and easier to stack for a dance or similar function. Popcorn and soda pop were sold for five and ten cents.

Donald saw more movies than I did because Collie was a good friend of his mother Rita, but he still had to pay to get in. He chuckles as he recalls being there for a western movie one evening when a family from away out in the country came in and sat down near him. One of the older men, who may have been at his first movie ever, became so engrossed in the movie he thought he was in it. In one scene where the good guy entered a vacant house and approached a room with the door open and the bad guy hiding behind it, the man jumped up and shouted, "Watch out, watch out, he's got a gun!" With that, the other patrons broke into snickers and laughter, and some hollered, "Sit down and shut up."

Chapter 35

Tracks

To Donald and me one of the constants in our young lives was the railway tracks, especially the Georgetown-Lake Verde line that ran almost past our front door. To us the rails were a never-ending balance beam, where we each chose a rail and side by side competed to see which one could walk the longest distance, without falling off or even touching the ground with one foot. We also ran as fast as we could between the rails, to see how many ties we could jump (our own version of the long jump, although we had never heard of it). Other times we walked along, kicking stones ahead of us, just because they were there, large and plenty, or we would simply pick one up and throw it at a sign, a post or a tree. Some days, if we were going across the bridge in the village, we walked around via the railway bridge just for fun, instead of the highway bridge, which was a shorter distance.

Both sides of the tracks had page wire fencing that we could easily climb over, especially near a post, up one side and down the other, no problem. One Sunday afternoon, in the springtime, when we were ten or eleven, Donald and I were playing down by the spring in Walsh's pond. We decided to go for a walk on the tracks, which were right beside us. At that time of year the tracks were used by many pedestrians, because the roads were so wet and muddy, and the tracks were high and dry. It was not uncommon for some country people to walk three or four miles into the village for a visit, and then walk back out on the tracks. During the previous winter, the section men from the railroad had cut all the small bushes along the tracks, using sharp axes, which left sharp slanted stumps, sticking up through the snow. As an annual exercise, later in the spring, the same men burned the grass along the tracks.

When I climbed the fence beside a post and got near the top, the post started to wobble. I lost my balance and fell forward, landing face down, with my hands supporting my upper body. My left shin, however, came down on one of those sharp stumps and cut the front of my leg. I got up, and Donald helped me walk back to my house, which was nearby. Daddy took me in the car to Dr. Sheppard, and he closed the gash with seven stitches. The doctor gave me strict orders to stay off the leg, as much as I could, and come back in a week to get the stitches out, which I did. Once again came orders from the doctor to take it easy and let the leg continue to heal. This time I didn't listen and kept on running, jumping and climbing trees. The wound opened up but, with Mom's care, didn't get infected. It left quite a scar, which I still have today. We later learned that the wobbly post had been partly burned off at the ground by the spring grass burning.

One of the railway vehicles that fascinated Donald and me was the pump trolley that the section foreman, Danny Birt, used to travel back and forth to work and sometimes to haul other men and supplies. He usually parked the trolley off the tracks near the crossing in front of our house. The trolley got its power from a chest-high bar that pivoted in the middle with handles at both ends. It was designed for two men standing on the deck, facing each other, but it could be operated by one man with considerably more effort. In the early days, Donald and I used to climb up on the deck, reach up and pull at the handles, but to no avail. There were also handles at either end of the deck, so that the trolley could be lifted on or off the track or turned around. One Sunday afternoon, when Donald and I got big enough, perhaps twelve or thirteen, we loaded the trolley onto the tracks, and took it for a spin out towards the Black Bridge, but the switch to that line was closed, so we reversed the trolley, came back and parked it. As far as we know, nobody saw us, and we never attempted that again.

Later, the pump trolley was replaced by one with a gasoline engine and two seats for driver and one passenger. Now that was riding to work in comfort. Donald and I never had ride on that one.

Steam train engine on the Pisquid black bridge

Mount Stewart train station

Chapter 36

The Trains

In 1925, when the CN railway on P.E.I. was completed, Mount Stewart became a railway junction. In 1941 Daddy went to work for the railroad and worked on trains all over the Island. At Mount Stewart trains coming from Charlottetown could, with the pull of a switch handle, go northeast to Souris and Elmira or Southeast to Montague and Georgetown. The Georgetown line had another switch about two miles South of Mount Stewart to a spur line that went to Lake Verde and terminated a few miles across the river from Charlottetown. Nearer to Georgetown was a second switch that gave access to another spur that terminated at Montague. This line was mostly a five mile downgrade, and when conditions were right Daddy as brakeman was known to ride on top of a box car disconnected from the train downhill all the way in to Montague. If needed, he had a wheel at the top of the ladder on the car that operated a brake to slow the car or stop it.

A regular train crew consisted of a driver or engineer,

a fireman, a conductor, a brakeman and a baggage man. Early trains were powered by steam engines, hence the need for a fireman to stoke the engine with coal to keep steam pressure up. Later, in the early 1970s, steam was replaced by diesel, but the fireman was still needed to watch the right hand side of the train and to send and receive signals from the brakeman on that side of the train. My Mom's eldest brother was an engineer on the steam engines, and her youngest brother was an engineer on the diesels.

With the exception of the Lake Verde run, all trains stayed overnight and on weekends at Souris, Georgetown and Tignish at the extremities of the Island. They ran six days a week, carrying passengers, mail and freight into Charlottetown in the morning and returning to the same town in the evening. They stopped at every whistle stop, picking up or dropping off mail, passengers, and freight, including full cream cans in the morning and empty cream cans in the evening. On the outskirts of Charlottetown there was another larger, busier junction at Royalty where trains could meet, stop, switch, back into the main station in the city, and depart via the same route.

In winter, the train might have a snow plough in front of the engine, and after a severe storm, a special plough train might be dispatched, made up of the engine, caboose and plough only.

One of Dad's first jobs on the railroad was shoveling snow as part of a crew after a storm so bad that the plough train couldn't get through some drifts. His first full-time job was baggage man which meant loading and unloading all items carried in the baggage car. As a rookie, he had little choice of which train he might be dispatched on or what hour of the day or night he might be working, especially if it was a special run. He also learned the job of brakeman, which consisted of assembling trains, shunting cars so that they would be easier to drop off, and signaling to the engineer and fireman in the engine. This task was tough enough in daylight and good weather, but very difficult after dark or in fog, heavy rain or snow storms. The longer the train and the more curves in the track, the greater the difficulty to send and receive signals.

At night time in his early years he signaled using a kerosene lantern with a clear or red glass and a cage. It was later replaced by a lantern with a battery and two bulbs. There were no two-way radios or cell phones, so if he couldn't get a signal straight, he would have to walk the length of the train to the engine to speak to the engineer or fireman.

In winter, the couplers and air hoses between the cars which had to be opened and closed manually might be frozen and caked with snow and ice, making them very difficult to disconnect. This might also be the case with some of the switches to sidings and the padlocks on them, but the brakeman was expected to persevere and get the job done. A brakeman had to have very strong arms and hands and be sure-footed, able to climb the ladders on cars, to walk or run on top of the cars and to jump on and off a moving train in all kinds of weather.

The Georgetown line ran within fifty yards of our house. When Daddy worked that train as baggageman, coming from the city in the evening, he would often throw a small brown paper bag of candy to us as the train went by. The bag would have a small piece of wood or coal tied to it to keep it from blowing away in the wind. As kids, we would race to be the first to reach the bag, open it and have the pick of the contents. If Donald happened to be there, he would run with us and share the loot.

Occasionally, on Saturdays, if Daddy left his car in Georgetown, one or two of us children would get the conductor's permission to board the train at Mount Stewart, ride to Georgetown and come home with him. This was usually an adventure, because we would ride in the baggage car with him and help sort parcels, mail bags and empty cream cans and move them over to the correct door before the next stop. On days when one of my sisters was not available, Donald would come with me. At Christmas and Easter the mail bags would be piled almost to the roof of the car, and we would sit or lay on them between stops and just enjoy the ride. We would almost fall asleep sometimes listening to the clickety-clack of the wheels on the rails.

Trains were an important means of transportation

those days, especially in the spring when the roads were bad, and when seed and fertilizer were coming in for the farmers. They were also important in the fall and winter, when potatoes and other produce were being shipped out.

Dad worked the railroad for thirty years before retiring in 1971. Within twenty years the trains on P.E.I. were also retired, replaced by transport trucks.

Chapter 37

'Goin Swimmin'

What's that? A spelling error? Not really, because, when we were young, both adults and children alike seldom pronounced the 'g' in any word ending in 'ing'. But that's not what this story is about.

In my early days as an adult, away from home in boot camp, we former islanders were ridiculed for not being able to swim by our new friends, who had been brought up in towns and cities. As children they had access to parks with swimming holes, community swimming pools, and instructors to teach them, but few rural people from our parents' generation could swim or even begin to teach us how. We had lots of open water, but just as we had no organized sports in our village, we were devoid of the opportunity to learn how to swim. Even commercial fishermen, who spent a lifetime on the water, as did their forefathers before them, were unable to swim. They are still being cajoled and encouraged by government and friends even to wear floatation devices on the water.

Barney and Me

Like those from generations before us, we looked forward to 'goin swimmin' in summer on the North shore of the Island and frolicking in the breakers from the Gulf of St. Lawrence. However, we never really learned how to swim, and even though our parents warned us about the undertow, we paid little heed until we got into trouble. Although none of us drowned in the undertow, some of us experienced the blind fear of going out too deep in rough water, unable to touch bottom and unable to swim. Fortunately, someone who could swim and heard us screaming for help was always there to rescue us, coughing and choking down gulps of salt water.

One summer afternoon in the village, when Daddy was home, he pumped up two old inner tubes and offered to take Donald and me down below the old wharf for a swim. I was probably eight and Donald seven years old. I forget what we wore for bathing suits, but we were covered. Donald and I each put an inner tube over our shoulder, and the three of us walked the short distance down to the river on the South side of the wharf. There was no sandy beach, just a muddy bottom. Daddy suggested that we wade out into the water, push the inner tubes out in front of us, and kick our feet like we were swimming. We were only to go out a little way, then turn around and come back.

Daddy stayed on the shore in knee-deep water. I'm not sure what Donald was doing, but before long I was climbing on top of my inner tube, feeling proud of myself floating along, until I noticed I was drifting farther out into the river towards deeper water. I couldn't reach the wharf beside me. I panicked and jumped off the inner tube, which popped out from under me. I cried out, clawed, kicked and choked the few feet to the wharf and hung on. Daddy couldn't swim, but he waded out almost up to his shoulders, grabbed me and carried me back to shore. That was the end of 'goin swimmin' that day, and it was the last time we ever went for a swim in the river. I'm sure Daddy never forgot it.

Later, when Donald was eleven and I was twelve, we both rode with other children on the back of Pumkin's truck six miles to the beach at Savage Harbour. Under the guidance of Red Cross instructors, on fine days for two weeks, we tried to learn how to float and do the dog paddle a short distance in the surf. I was given a Beginner's Badge at the end of the course. I really learned to swim at age eighteen in boot camp. Donald told me he learned to swim in the river at the age of twelve or thirteen out of sheer desperation, when other boys his age were swimming and an older boy threw him off the wharf. Afterwards, Reggie told Donald if he hadn't been able to swim, he would have jumped in and saved him. Donald later said, jokingly, "That was little consolation to me as I flew through the air and hit the water."

Chapter 38

Here Comes Winter

Almost all the old houses on the block and in the rest of the village had no concrete foundation and little or no insulation. So, each fall, as winter approached, the number one priority was to stop the draughts, to keep the cold out and the heat in. Many chores had to be done, and all the older children pitched in.

The first task was to bank the house. We would gather together all the wide boards we could find, maybe some from last year. If there weren't enough, we'd have to add new ones. Those who could handle an axe would sharpen some small wooden stakes to hold the boards in place, approximately ten inches from the wall of the house. Then we'd take the horse and cart or borrow a half ton truck and go to the mill to get some sawdust or shavings, anything to trap the air and keep the cold out. We'd do that on all sides of the house, leaving only the doorways open. In later years, when more pick-up trucks were available and fewer sawmills, sawdust was replaced by seaweed, because it was plentiful on the bay shore at

Canavoy, and it could be stored and used again the next year.

Next, we'd go to the barn floor or loft and dig out the storm windows, saved from last year, check for broken panes, line them against an outside wall, and wash them with soap and water. Then we would look for marks on each storm window to identify where it went on the house and hope it would fit. Also we'd look for a can with screws or fasteners, still there from last year, to hold the windows tightly in place and install them on ground floor windows. We had storm windows for three bedroom windows only on the upstairs of our side of the house and none for the upstairs on the rented side. As a teenager, I slept in the spare bedroom on that side, to keep my grandmother company, and most winter mornings I could scrape the frost off the inside of the window pane with my thumb nail.

Next we'd locate three storm doors, one for the front and two for the back, clean the cob webs off, paint them if necessary, check the hinges and latches and install them. Our house already had a sun porch outside the kitchen door, and in later years Daddy built a small three-sided wooden porch over the front door for added shelter from the storms. It was temporary, had a door with a small window, and was taken down each spring and stored in the barn.

To add extra heating capacity for both sides of our house, we had two winter stoves stored in the barn or woodshed, complete with lengths of stove pipe that had to be cleaned by tapping the sides with a small piece of wood to knock the soot out. Perhaps they needed replacement or a fresh coat of paint, depending on how hot they had been the previous winter. Winter stoves came in all shapes and sizes. The smallest and cheapest was the queen heater that burned wood only, but it was the most lethal, because the top, bottom and sides were made of thin gauge metal. If the fire was stoked too much or banked for the night, it could overheat until the sides and top grew red, and it regularly caused chimney fires. If the overheating was not detected in time, the house would catch fire and burn down, sometimes with people in it. That did happen over the years in many parts of Canada. Smoke detectors hadn't yet been invented. We had a queen heater in the dining room one winter, but never again, for these very reasons.

We also had a tall, elegant looking stove that burned hard nut coal only. The hopper for the coal was on top of the stove, and it had to be poured in with a special coal bucket that had a snout on it to guide the coal in. This was a job for adults only. That stove was the most efficient and held fire all night, but it was the most expensive, because of the cost of the special coal it needed.

The last winter stove we had before we got an oil furnace was a furnacette. It had a cast iron body and a chrome grill on top and was by far the biggest and heaviest. We needed two very strong men or four adults, one on each corner, to carry it into and out of the house. It would take large hardwood blocks that burned all night and still had hot coals in the morning. Our winter stove was set up in the dining room, with a grill in the ceiling to allow heat into the upstairs. All winter stoves were set up with the appropriate heat shields, both on the floor and nearby wall. Grandmother's winter stove was compact and durable and sat in the living room. It didn't hold fire overnight and had to be lit each morning.

More stoves required more fuel, so more trips to the mill for slabs, and more orders for hardwood from the country. No matter where it came from, we still had to stack it in the woodsheds, as high as the roof if necessary.

I had lots of help from my Uncle Wilfred in stocking grandmother's woodshed. He used to stop in every trip he visited his mother, helping to cut kindling and split hardwood. If he had time, he'd fill the wood box in her back porch. He was my favourite uncle. When both winter stoves were all set up, we'd light a fire in them to make sure everything worked okay and also burn any excess paint off the pipes.

Francis Rose delivered our hardwood cut in stove lengths and split if ordered. He used a wagon or bob-sleighs with a box, pulled by a light team of horses that looked as round as bottles, so much so that the breech-ings slid half way up their rump.

One day in our yard, I complimented Francis on the excellent shape his team was in. Francis smiled and said,

"I can't get by on three meals a day, so every night before I go to bed, I go to the barn to check on them and give them each half a can of oats."

When you live on an island the wind rarely, if ever, stops blowing, so close-by shelter is important, especially in the extremes of winter. The object of personal comfort is always to get out of the weather if at all possible, into barns where there might be heat from animals, horse sheds, wood sheds, the rink shack where there might be a fire in the stove, Grampy's workshop where there might also be a fire going, the forge where there would be heat from the hearth, even snow forts where the heat from our own bodies would improve the temperature. For two small boys like Donald and me, going home to our houses was usually the last resort, because our Mom's would be busy, our sisters scrubbing the floor with greetings like, "Take those boots off" or "Don't track that snow in here."

My sister Miriam, eight years younger than me, remembers one day that I rushed in the front door and upstairs to the bathroom with my rubber boots on. My eldest sister Eileen was scrubbing the hall floor downstairs and hollered at me to take my boots off. I stopped abruptly at the top of the stairs and said, "You want my boots off, okay, here." With that, I loosened one boot partly off my foot to kick it down the stairs. I must have leaned into the kick a bit too hard, because the boot sailed through air and took out one of three window panes in the front door. She was not pleased, and

177

neither was Mom, because I can't remember if I ever did get to the bathroom that day, or even the event itself, but I don't doubt Miriam's memory, even for a minute. It sounds like something I would do.

There were also fun times in the winter too, like building snow forts and having snow ball fights with other kids. Which reminds me, once in early spring when the snow was all gone from the school yard, at recess, some of us jumped over the fence into the neighbour's yard, where there was snow enough for a quick snow ball fight. The yard belonged to one of the merchants in the village, not just an ordinary Joe. When the principal found out, he lined us up, ordered us to hold out our hands, and he slapped each one of them once with a leather belt that he kept in his desk for that purpose. His nickname was 'Mighty', and we got what we called 'gettin the strap'. It was the only time Donald and I ever got the strap.

Chapter 39

'Fishin Eels'

Donald never went with me, but every early winter when I was between seven and eleven and the river started to freeze over, Grampy invited me to go with him fishing eels on the upper part of the river called the 'S'. It was aptly named because of the obvious shape of the river at that location.

When the day arrived, a Saturday usually, we gathered the eel spear with its extra long wooden shaft from the rafters of Grampy's workshop, a small axe, and a heavy burlap bag. We were both dressed in warm winter clothes. I wore my gum boots, heavy pants, wool mitts and a cap with ear lugs. Grampy wore felt boots with rubber bottoms, winter pants, a heavy jacket and a tweed cap. He chose the time to go because he didn't want the ice to get too thick and make it harder to cut. He usually carried the spear and the axe, and I carried the empty bag.

Off we went on foot, out the back lane, along the tracks to the railway bridge. After we tested the river ice for safety, we crept out onto it and walked to the 'S' about a quarter mile away. On the way, Grampy told me that in winter eels hibernate in the mud at the river bottom, making them easier to catch.

Once Grampy got his bearings, he would find a spot with a reachable depth of water in the same general area where he'd caught eels in previous years. Some years the ice was so clear we could almost see the river bottom. He'd drop the spear, pick up the axe and cut a circular hole in the ice approximately eighteen inches in diameter. The piece he cut out, usually no more than two inches thick, was pushed out of the way under the ice. Then he took the spear with its fan shaped business end and its six steel hooks on springy, pencil-sized eight inch long shafts. The hooks faced inward toward a one inch flat steel divider. The spear was designed to be poked into the muddy river bottom, to catch an eel between the front of one hook and the back of the next, holding it there long enough to be pulled out through the hole in the ice. Grampy started the spear in a wide circle, holding the shaft at a slant and gradually bringing it upright, herding the eels into the center of the circle, in the river bottom, making them easier to catch.

He had a 'D' handle on his end of the spear shaft, so he could drive the spear firmly and quickly into the mud, then yank it back even faster. If he struck something solid, he could feel it in the shaft and quickly pull the spear, hand over hand out of the hole in the ice, to lessen the chance of the prey escaping. Sometimes it was only a stick or debris from the bottom of the river. He knew when he hooked into an eel by the vibration in the spear shaft, especially if it was a big one. When he shook the eel off the spear and it hit the ice, my job was to corral it and put it wriggling into the burlap bag. I had to be quick to grab and hang onto the eel, hold the mouth of the bag open with the other hand, and not let the others escape while I deposited the new one. I was happy to have my wool mitts, because the eels were slippery, and I'd never be able to hold them with my bare hands. Besides, my hands would be too cold. Now and then, one would fall too close to the hole and escape.

A slogan taught to us in school for safety on early winter ice was, "One inch, keep off; two inches, one may; three inches, small groups; four inches okay." Grampy never did learn that slogan. He was tall, well built, in good shape for his age, weighing almost 200 pounds, but he thought only of ice that would be easy to cut holes in. It always worried me as I watched him circling the hole and pulling eels out as an ever deepening pool of water formed around his feet. If he had ever fallen in, I could never have saved him. The best I could have done was run for help to the nearest house a half-mile away. No cell phones, no 911. Thank God it never happened.

When one hole was fished out, Grampy moved over to a dryer spot and cut another hole. He continued fishing and cutting holes until the bag had what he thought was enough eels for the day. Then we'd pick up and head home, me carrying the axe, he the spear and the bag of eels.

His work wasn't done when we got home. After a cup of Grammie's tea and a biscuit for both of us, he started to skin the eels to get them ready for the frying pan. One at a time, he'd take the eels out of the bag in the workshop, hang them up by the gills on the same hook he hung the foxes to skin them. With a sharp knife he'd cut the skin all the way around below the head. Then he'd tear a small strip of skin away from the body, trapping it between his thumb and the side of his knife blade. Slowly, steadily, he'd pull the entire skin down the body to the tail, much like you'd take a sock off a sweaty foot, then he'd cut the skin off the body and discard it. He'd take the sometimes still wiggling body down from the hook, cut the head off, throw it to the assembled cats, and drop the body into a bucket of clean water. This would be repeated as many times as needed to skin the contents of the bag. Never once did he ever offer to let me try to fish with the spear or to skin an eel. I probably wouldn't have been able to do it anyway. Later, I'd be invited to join him and Grammie for a feast of eels, but I would graciously decline and go home next door to Mom's cooking.

Ice fishing for eels

Chapter 40

Airplanes and Snowmobiles

During wartime, the influence of airplanes was prevalent in the village, night and day, because of a pilot training base at the Charlottetown airport some fifteen miles down the river. The pilots used the river as a guide for practice flights in the daytime and flares along the river at night to practice night flying as well as flying low over the water. In daylight sometimes the planes flew so low that we could clearly see the pilots in the cockpit. Luckily none of them crashed, at least not near our village.

Most nights there were two large oil-burning pot flares burning on the wharves. The wharves were made of creosote treated lumber, and they occasionally caught fire from the flares. That would alert the small village volunteer Fire Department, which had only a hand-me-down hose reel that could be hooked up to a water pump driven by a small gasoline engine. It was mounted on a two wheel cart pulled by two men and had some metal buckets with ropes on them to throw into the river and get water as an alternative for putting the fire out.

Barney and Me

Some nights the sirens would signal a practice black-out, which meant lights out in all houses and shops and all window blinds closed tightly if a light was needed inside. We were told this was in preparation for a possible air raid. To us children this was a fearful exercise at first, but later on we saw it as a chance to tease each other and play in the dark with our siblings.

The influence of airplanes also brought to the village our first snowmobile built by our only car dealer, Danny Mullins. It was a capsule-like two-seater sitting high on two skis like a giant ostrich and driven by an engine with a rear propeller and a rudder for steering. Donald and I never got a ride in it, but we stood with others on a clear, cold, windy, winter day and marveled at its speed and its maneuverability on the river ice. Stories abounded about its use and flexibility as well as future possibilities, and there was even one about the local doctor being delivered quickly to an emergency call.

We did get a ride later in the next snowmobile acquired by Mr. Mullins. It was the first-ever Bombardier in the village, a mini-bus with cat tracks on rubber tires, wheels under the main body and two large skis in front mounted on hydraulic springs for comfort and steering. It had two front doors for the driver and one passenger and one large side door for cargo and other passengers. It had portable benches along both side walls inside. What a thrill to go flying over deep snow drifts and down the river ice in that 'new spaceship of the day'.

185

Chapter 41

'Hitchin Rides'

When Donald and I were nine or ten on a mild winter evening with big wet snow flakes sticking to our faces, we would be down on Main Street in front of his house just looking for something to do. We probably should have been home doing chores or homework, but this was more fun.

Most of the winter there was always an inch or two of hard packed snow on Main Street from car traffic because salt was rarely used. Coupled with the fresh snow it made for excellent sledding or just running and sliding on the car tracks. Should a slow moving car approach, we'd act nonchalant or hide behind a snow bank, and as the car passed we'd run after it, grab the rear bumper, brace ourselves and slide along on our gum boots until one of us fell or another car approached from behind. We'd roll off, jump into a snow bank, laugh at the fun we were having and wait for another slow car to come by. We had the advantage because we were short enough and crouched down so the driver couldn't spot us in the rear view mirror, and the street lights were at least one hundred yards apart. Also, at that time, few cars had an outside rear view mirror, and if there was one, it was on the driver's side only.

We rarely stayed with one car for more than a minute or two, because our hands would get cold with wet mitts on steel bumpers. We also never went across the bridge, because the center span was usually bare, and there was more traffic on the other side. Sometimes the exhaust from older cars, if the engine was burning oil, was simply too much, so we'd let go and wait for another, preferably going in the opposite direction. The stretch of the street we used the most was from the end of the Peakes Road to the center span of the bridge, close to home, in case we had to make a break for it. There was always the risk we'd slide through some fresh, partly frozen horse buns, but we'd just laugh and brush it off.

Chapter 42

The Rink

The Mount Stewart rink was outdoors with natural ice that had to be shoveled, swept and flooded by hand before anyone could use it. Located behind the Clark's wagon shed on the edge of the marsh beside the river not far from the north wharf, it was directly across the river from our house and visible from a kitchen window, even at night, because it had two strands of light bulbs running from one end to the other. It also had a rink shack with a wood and coal burning stove and benches around the walls where we could sit to change our skates or take a rest. It even had a sound system that played music on 78 records during public skating, especially at night, songs like "Let Me Call You Sweetheart", "With Someone Like You" and "Cruising Down the River". I can still hear the sound of the music crackling over the lone speaker as we skated together, more or less in circles, on a frosty night. On a calm night, we could easily hear the music from our back yard across the river. Many bashful young boys got their first flicker of romance skating to that music with their favorite girl. Some older boys were known to continue the same pursuit in the rink shack after everyone else had gone home, especially if the lights had been turned out.

The rink had boards about three feet high around it and a gate at the rink shack to enter and exit. There was heavy wire mesh above the boards at both ends to stop stray pucks from being lost in the snow outside until spring. When you grew taller than the boards, it was an experience you'd never forget, having your face shoved, accidentally or otherwise, into that wire mesh.

After a winter storm it was not uncommon to have snow drifts inside the rink higher than the boards in some places. Volunteers had to be conscripted and all available shovels borrowed, hopefully with the owner attached. All able bodied men, women and children were welcome. Our access to the rink was governed by how much we helped to get it ready in the first place. When the high tides would come into the river every month, the corner of the rink nearest the wharf would flood with partial salt water, leaving a yellowish, elevated slushy mess. That had to be removed when it thawed, and re-flooded when the temperature dropped again.

Young boys did not have a hockey team, and girl's hockey was unheard of. The older boys and young men had sort of a team that would play the occasional game against another team from outside the village. Equipment consisted of skates and stick, maybe gloves or mitts, and parts of Eaton's catalogues as shin pads. One team might have a goalie with old goalie pads and glove if he was lucky. There were no referees.

If we younger boys wanted to play, we were allowed, by invitation, to play 'shinny' with older boys and some younger men. One afternoon during one such game, I was knocked down in front of the net, and as I hit the ice I was struck in the mouth by the puck, shot by one of the bigger boys. The shot broke one of my upper front teeth diagonally so that only a sharp tusk remained. My upper lip was smashed and bled profusely.

I don't remember exactly what happened after that because I was dazed and in shock. I think Donald was there that day. Someone helped me up and gave me some snow to put on my mouth and sent me home with my skates still on. I met my younger sister on the bridge. I was crying and holding my mouth. She asked a sympathetic, "What happened?" I just kept on walking and mumbled a not-so-nice, "Get out of my way."

At home Mom checked the tooth, phoned the dentist, Dr. Redden, and took me back across the bridge to see him. He saved the tooth and later put a temporary cap on it, and even later he gave me a permanent cap with a gold back and filled in the front with white porcelain where the piece was missing. That broken piece was never found, and I've had three crowns on that same tooth since.

At the rink, pucks were at a premium and rarely new,

mostly souvenirs from games at the Forum in the city or from one of the few covered rinks then operating on the island. There were no buckets of pucks for practice. In fact, there were no practices. We learned as we played, both good habits and bad. Some pucks were so old they had chunks out of them, and the rubber was so hard and dry it was almost petrified. It may have been lost in a snow bank outside the rink, baked in the summer sun, and found its way back to the rink the following winter. Most pucks had identifying marks put on them by their owners so they could be reclaimed after a game. I had one new puck, probably a gift in my Christmas stocking. I burned my initials into one side of it with a hot poker from the kitchen stove. They were so large and deep, they covered the whole side of the puck.

During a game, the standing rule was that if you shot the puck over the boards into the snow, you had to climb over, skates and all, maybe up to your waist in snow, and retrieve it. If the snow was hard, the puck might be resting on top, and you might not have to go too far to get it. If the snow was soft, the puck would disappear into the snow, and you'd use your stick to poke around until you hit something solid. If you were lucky, it was the puck, and you could dig it out. Otherwise you kept digging, because that might be the only puck at the rink that day. If some other players became impatient or took pity on you, they might climb over the boards and join in the hunt. If nobody found it and no one else had a puck, the game was over for that day, unless someone walked home, probably on his skates (no skate guards) and got one. Then the game continued until everyone had enough.

Outdoor skating

Pisquid black bridge

Chapter 43

Skating to Pisquid

Once or twice a winter, after a January thaw followed by a freeze, Donald and I would lace up our skates, take our hockey sticks, tie our boots together, hang them around our necks and head downriver about two and a half miles to visit a family of five boys who lived on a farm overlooking the Pisquid River. The boys ranged in age from a bit older than us to some way younger.

On the way there, we would skate under the railway bridge that everyone called the Black Bridge, built entirely of wooden creosote pilings and timbers. Usually it was not enough simply to skate under the bridge, but we had to spin around a couple of pilings before continuing on our way. If we were lucky, it would be a cool clear day with the wind on our backs, but it could also be bitterly cold with the wind in our faces.

When we got to our destination, Glendon Jay and some of his four younger brothers, all cousins of mine, might be down at the river skating and playing shinny with some neighbour boys. If not, we would take our skates off, put on our boots, tie our skates around our necks and hike up through the fields a quarter mile to the house.

I'm sure the boys' mother shuddered when she saw us coming, but she would invite us in, give us some biscuits or cookies to eat and something to drink, and away we'd go, back outside to resume our fun. If the weather was bad, we would visit the big barn with the horses and cows and the smaller barns, each with pigs, hens, or sheep all inside for the winter. If it was near feeding time, we might take turns on the crank of the turnip slicer for the cows, and when it stopped we could sample a choice slice of cold turnip. I know that doesn't sound enticing on a cold winter day, but when you're young with hollow legs, it really tasted good. And we'd have a handful of bran right out of the bag for dessert.

If the boys' father was home and allowed it, we might take one of the horses out into the yard with just a bridle and a short rope for a rein and try to ride it bareback. Our favorite horse was Polly. Most of the farm boys knew how to ride, so they would lead the horse over to a fence so Donald or I could climb up onto its back. They took great pleasure when the horse would suddenly move sideways, and we would land in a heap on the ground. Polly would just stand there and look down at us with a disgusted glance.

When we ran out of things to do around the farm and if it was still daylight, some of us might return to the river, put on our skates and have a little game. Donald and I would try to watch our time so we could make it home before dark, but more than once we would be guided home on the last leg of our journey by the lights from the village. Our worried mothers, after a short scolding, would still feed us our supper. We'd have no trouble getting to sleep that night with visions of the day still running through our heads.

In summer, Donald and I would walk the Lake Verde railway line across the same Black Bridge, which was not a long bridge, perhaps two hundred yards, and had two balconies on it that each housed a forty-five gallon metal drum filled with water in case of fire. We always assured ourselves that if the train came while we were on the bridge, we'd run to one of the balconies and stay there until the train passed. That never happened. After we crossed the bridge we walked a short distance to the end of the MacKinnon Point Road and down it to the same farm to visit the same family of boys that we visited in the winter.

If there was work to be done like going for the cows in the field or helping to milk, we would pitch in, and afterwards we would go for a walk or dream up some silly game of chase or go into a nearby field and have a pickup baseball game. That is, if there was a bat and ball available. If anyone had a ball glove, it was a luxury. When the afternoon was done, Donald and I would go out to the road and try to hitch a ride back to the village. If not, we'd walk back the same way we came.

During the winter of one of those adolescent years, age ten or eleven, one of us had heard or read about a thing called an ice boat that was driven by a sail, so we decided we would build one and sail it on the river ice. We gathered some scraps of lumber including two fairly long 2x4s and made a cross out of them. Then we rummaged through closets, attics and barn lofts to find three old skates. We separated the boots from the blades and converted the blades to runners for our ice boat. We also borrowed what was most likely someone's clothesline pole for the mast and an old piece of canvas for a sail. We spiked and nailed the 2x4s together and attached the three skate blades to the bottom side, one on the extreme right end, one to the extreme left end, and one to the rear, which we rigged so it would swivel like a rudder to permit steering. We drilled a hole at the intersection of the cross, stuck the base of the mast in it, and supported it with guide wires. I can't remember how we fastened the canvas for the sail, and I don't recall receiving help from adults to build our ice boat, but we may well have.

On a windy winter Saturday when the ice wasn't too rough, we carried the finished project down to the river below the two wharves and set it on the ice. We lined it up with the wind at our backs and hoisted the sail. The boat took off. We both ran after it and tried to get on, only to realize that we had forgotten to install seats.

197

The 2x4's had little room even for our small behinds, so we ended up lying on the ice, laughing our fool heads off, hanging onto the boat as it dragged us along. After we managed to stop, we dragged the boat back to the shore, never did put seats on it, and can't remember what became of it, probably firewood.

Chapter 44

Harvesting Ice

In the days before refrigerators, some homes, though not ours, had ice boxes to keep food cool in summer. Other homes had ice houses, separate buildings which stored large blocks of ice packed in sawdust to keep the ice from melting. The ice was harvested from any fresh water pond that was easily accessible on fine days late in winter, when the ice was at least sixteen inches thick. It was cut by hand into rectangular blocks with a special long ice saw that had a handle on one end, or with a cross cut saw modified for the purpose. Each block would weigh thirty to forty pounds and would float in the water when cut free from the pack. Men and young men used one foot to push the block down into the water and when it bobbed back up they would grab it with a special pair of long-handled ice tongs and drag it out onto the ice. They would then load it onto a horse drawn sleigh to be hauled to an ice house.

The sleigh would have a wooden board deck with 2x4s spiked around the outside to keep the blocks from sliding off en route. When the sleigh was loaded, some of the men would stay at the pond cutting ice while a young man would drive the horse and load home to the ice house. There another adult would help to unload the ice and stack it into the ice house, layering the ice with sawdust as insulation from the summer heat and ease of separation when a single block was needed.

Donald and I, as village kids, were not directly involved in this work, but on Saturdays, when the harvest was in full swing, we walked to Desi's dam north of the village to watch. The dam was originally built by the railway about a quarter mile above the junction in the village to supply water to the tower on the Souris siding where steam locomotives could top up with water for their next trip. The dam was also a good place for us to go skating in winter and trout fishing in summer. Donald and I did both and enjoyed them immensely whenever we could get there. It was North and East of the village above the St. Peter's highway and most days a little too far for us to walk.

When we arrived at the dam we were warned to stay back from the hole for fear of falling in. If we were lucky, we'd hitch a ride with a friend going with a load of ice to a nearby ice house and help unload if we could, then hitch a ride back to the pond. Most drivers used a horse rug or a burlap bag with straw stuffed in it as a cushion to sit on top of the load for the trip. If it was a rug, there'd be room on it for Donald and me. If not, then we'd stand on the side of the sleigh and hold on to a stake.

On one such trip, on a steep incline, the load shifted, and two blocks slid off the back of the sleigh. Preston stopped the horse, and one of us stood by his head while Preston loaded the blocks back onto the sleigh. The rope reins were long enough that Preston could cut a piece off them with his pocket knife and tie it between the two back stakes to keep the blocks on the load for the rest of the trip.

This ice cutting bee was repeated over a period of weeks until everyone had all the ice they needed for the coming summer. Some of the ice was harvested commercially and sold to fish plants in other parts of the island for use the following summer.

Our family used an abandoned well in my grandfather's back yard to keep food, especially milk and butter, cool during the summer. Two of my uncles and one grandfather had ice houses, and what a chore it was in summer to help dig a block of ice out of the sawdust, break it away from adjacent blocks, brush it off, place it on something clean and carry it over to the house. Then we had to help break it into small pieces to put in the ice box or to pack around the cylinder that made homemade ice cream, and later we would share the finished product.

Chapter 45

Horse Racing on River Ice

In winter, the ice on the river below the wharves was also the scene of horse races, weather and work permitting. Men and horses from the village and surrounding areas gathered in all kinds of conveyances, mostly in sleighs and two wheeled carts. A race was a straight one quarter mile dash with the start and finish marked off by small evergreen bushes previously frozen into the ice. Other men, women and children would turn out to stand or sit on sleighs to watch and cheer on their favorite horse and driver. It was an event that only happened two or three times a winter, mostly on Saturday afternoons, and the reward to the winner was simply bragging rights. I cheered for my cousin Buddy and his horse Jack who pulled a driving sleigh and who was normally Dell's teammate.

Jack had some standardbred racing blood in him, but his best record was not on the ice, rather it was on the road. Buddy lived six miles from the village. One night, he and Jack picked up his Aunt Cora at the railway station in the village and headed home. When Cora got into the sleigh, unknown to Buddy, she looked at her watch, and eighteen minutes later they arrived in Buddy's yard in Savage Harbour. Not bad for an ordinary farm horse, don't you think?

Freezing bushes into the ice, or 'bushing the ice' as it was called, was for more than just horse races. It was also to mark the ice so travellers could find their way in a snow storm or at night so they didn't wander off the beaten path and get into a spring hole or open water where the river met the land. Bushing the ice was an annual event on the rivers and bays after freeze up when the ice became thick enough to carry everybody. Men with horses and sleighs loaded with small spruce trees went out onto the ice and used a crowbar or axe to punch or chop a hole in the ice, where they inserted a small tree into the water and slush and packed snow around it to prop it up until it froze in. This was repeated many times with bushes thirty or forty yards apart in a mostly straight line to fashion a trail to be followed for the rest of the winter. When a team ran out of bushes, they would go back to the woods and get some more until their section was completed or they met another team doing the same thing. Neighbours on both ends continued planting trees in the ice over a number of days until the ice highways were completed. The main one stretched from the head of the river to Charlottetown, some twenty miles, but other rivers, bays and harbours were also bushed where needed.

When the ice was deemed strong enough, cars also travelled on the ice, mostly in daytime. One mild spring day, Daddy was returning from the city in his car, driving on the river ice near Scotchfort, and he drove through some surface water that splashed up onto the engine and caused it to stall. I wasn't with him, but Mom and my sister Connie were. He walked to a nearby farm and enlisted the farmer to bring his horse down to the river and tow the car off the ice. He was afraid to leave the car there overnight in case the ice melted and the car went to the river bottom. They probably hitched a ride home with someone from Fanningbrook and retrieved the car the next day.

Chapter 46

Milkman

When we lived on the farm, and for a time when we were first in the village, we had milk from our own cows, and of course, we also had all the work that went with it. Later in the village Dad got rid of the milk cows, and we started to get our milk from the milkman, Addison Coffin. He had a horse and wagon in the summer and the same horse pulling a sleigh in winter. She was a mare that was with foal almost every year. Over time, Addison raised at least four big handsome black horses from that mare. In fact, two of them were the lead team on one chain when they moved Danny Birt's house.

The milk came in round, heavy glass quart milk bottles with a flat, thin cardboard stopper that fit inside the rim at the top of the bottle. These stoppers were equipped with a tab to help in removing them. In the city, they had the name of the dairy stamped on them. The milk was whole, not pasteurized, and when the bottle was left sitting for a while, the cream came to the top, usually filling the neck of the bottle. Some mornings, after a severely cold winter night, if the full bottle was left in the back porch or in a snow bank, the frozen cream could be seen sticking up two inches above the top of the bottle, with the stopper sitting on top like a tiny hat. It was nature's instant ice cream cone. Then the challenge to the housewife was to keep the kids clear and save the cream from falling off the bottle as she brought the bottle into the kitchen. Most mothers had plenty of experience in handling such situations.

In summer at our house, the milk bottles were placed in a metal bucket with butter and other perishables and lowered on a rope into an abandoned twenty foot deep well in grandfather's back yard to be kept cool. The well was shared with two other families, each with their own bucket. You can imagine the commotion when one bucket hooked another during the raising or lowering and caused one to tip and spill the contents. When we became old enough and strong enough to lift the plank lid that covered the well, there were daily warnings not to get tangled up with the other buckets. I remember only one incident where there was a spill, not by me, but I did see the film of white on the stagnant water in the bottom of the well.

In spite of no ice house or ice box and the somewhat primitive methods for keeping perishable food edible in summer, we all grew up strong and healthy.

Chapter 47

Moving Danny Birt's House

In April, 1952, Danny Birt, the railway Section Foreman from Pisquid West, completed his plan to move his three storey house up the Hillsboro River to the village. The house was complete with front and back porches and two chimneys weighing an estimated thirty tons. Danny recruited the local farmers to bring their work horses to haul his house almost two miles over the river ice to the village. Some brought a single horse and teamed it with another single, and some farmers brought a team of two. Danny had earlier contracted a crew of men to raise the house up off its original foundation and place it on two giant wooden skids to slide it over the snow and ice. He also engaged a man with a horse and a capstain to move the house off the lot, down to the end of MacKinnon Point Road, over the railroad tracks and onto the river ice. Being a railroad foreman likely expedited his permission to cross the tracks.

On the appointed morning, the farmers brought a total of twelve teams, twenty-four horses, to move the house up the river ice to the village. It was a normal April day, clear and cold after a thaw, with a few snowflakes in the air. Each of the two skids under the house had a large logging chain attached to the front of it which would run between each of six teams up to the lead team. Some of the single horses were teamed with a horse they had never seen before, and the two owners agreed which one would drive the team during the trip. The single-tree or 'swing' behind each horse was fastened to a green hard-wood double-tree which in turn was fastened at intervals to the chain with heavy brace wire. The neck yoke of some teams was also attached to the chain to support its weight and to keep the team together. The driver of each team walked beside it on the outside of the line, and some teamsters carried an axe to cut their team free if the house went through the ice. Only a few adults and very few children knew of this venture, but in the morning rumors abounded in school about what was happening. When we got out of school at dinner time, we all could see the house sitting half way up the river bank below its intended destination on the southern outskirts of the village.

The students begged the teachers, and the teachers appealed to the principal, and we were let out early to go and see the house moved the rest of the way across the marsh, over the railway and the highway, to its final resting place. Donald and I went too, but the move didn't happen that day. We heard that shortly after the house got moving across the ice that morning, as it crossed the junction of the Pisquid and Hillsboro Rivers, one skid stared to break through the ice. At that location the ice would have been thinner due to the fast moving water underneath. As the house started to tip to one side, the only thing that averted disaster was the long cross timbers that extended out under the back porch. As the ends touched the ice, they took some of the weight off that skid. The horses, under extreme urging from the drivers, and with a tremendous effort from all teams, were able to keep the house moving until it righted itself on solid ice. The teamsters who had carried axes to cut the double trees to free their horses were grateful that they didn't have to use them.

On arrival on the river bank near the village, the men and horses took a well deserved break. The horses were disconnected from the chains and taken to barns or other shelter for a rest and something to eat. Here we should mention that during the trip and the break the tide was going out, which left the back end of the house on the ice lower than the front end on the river bank. And because of the frigid temperature, the skids had also frozen in.

By the time we got there, the men were hooking up the horses to the chains, but when they tried several times to move the house, it wouldn't budge. Besides, some of the horses, not being matched teams, were not pulling together. Also, the teamsters suspected that the shoulders of some of the horses had been 'gaulled' when the house almost went through the ice. So everyone agreed that they had done all they could do for the day and packed up and went home. As the crowd dispersed, Donald looked up at the house and said, "Looks like she may have to spend the night right here." It was said later that only one teamster, who probably had the finest team there that day, sent Danny a bill for his services. We don't know if he ever got paid.

Enter again the capstain and the single horse and driver. A capstain is a winch on a platform that is anchored to the ground ahead of a heavy object that has to be moved. A heavy rope or cable is wound around the winch, which sits on end and is turned by a horse or ox walking around it in circles. The animal is attached to a long bar or pole extending from the top of the winch, and the progress of the horse tightens the rope or cable attached to the object and moves it forward. This was a very slow and painstaking procedure, because each time the object came close to the capstain the assembly had to be moved ahead, anchored, and the procedure repeated again and again until the move was finished. Little by little, over a number of days, the house was moved across the marsh, over the tracks and the highway to its final resting place where it still stands today. Donald and I walked out the road or railway tracks most evenings to check its progress until it reached its destination.

Moving Danny Birt's House

Horse drawn box sleigh

Chapter 48

'Jumpin Ice Cakes'

When spring came and the ice in the river thawed, the river ice would gradually break up, compounded by extreme spring tides caused by the different phases of the moon. The break occurred even more quickly between the two bridges and the wharves. Donald and I watched the changes, including faster currents in the river, and we'd be ready to go 'jumpin ice cakes'.

First, smaller cakes of ice would break away from the pack out in the river, drift away with the tides, and eventually dissolve. These were dangerous to jump, even close to the shore, because they couldn't support our weight, especially if we stopped on one, but if we ran from one to another, they would only partially sink, and our momentum would carry us to a bigger one. If we missed, we'd get wet, but we'd manage to crawl up onto another larger cake of ice. We never even came close to drowning. We were fully clothed for early spring, including rubber boots with a good grip on them, but when we got wet, we also got cold. We weren't far from home if we needed a change of clothes, and we got better at it once we got our timing down.

Our mothers would plead and sometimes threaten us, but we couldn't resist the chance to go jumpin ice cakes. During the week, short days, school and chores would interfere, but we could still look forward to the weekends.

The largest and thickest ice cakes were always near the river bank, and when the incoming tide would peak we used a large pole to pry a selected cake away from shore as the tide lifted it. Donald and I learned early how to read the tides in the river so we could tell when the incoming tide would slow, peak and turn. We would then steer the larger ice cakes to open water, where we could hop on and go for a ride. An ice cake that would carry us safely and that we could handle might be five feet long, three or four feet wide and eight to ten inches thick. We would each have a long wooden pole that could reach bottom close to shore but not out in the channel. The outgoing water from under the highway bridge did not all go directly out between the two wharves. Some of it on our side of the river glanced off the South wharf and came back around towards the highway bridge. This created a large gentle whirlpool which, if we were lucky, would take us several times around.

One year, on a beautiful spring day, we managed to free and float a cake about seven or eight feet long and four to five feet wide. We stored it locked in close to shore and went home, where we got two wooden kitchen chairs with the backs off them from our barn and a couple of comic books. We loaded them onto our big ice cake, and as the tide rose, we floated it out into the whirlpool. This was the scene that greeted passers-by on the bridge – the two of us sitting on our chairs reading comic books and 'cruisin the river' around by the wharf and back again. Our cruise ended abruptly when someone told our mothers. We were definitely in the dog house, but to this day I can't remember our punishment. It couldn't have been too bad. "Could either one of you swim?" you might ask. "Not a stroke," we'd have to reply. It wouldn't have mattered anyway. Considering the ice cold water and us fully clothed, we probably wouldn't have survived.

Chapter 49

Trout and Gaspereaux

Later every spring, when the ice was gone from the river, the trout fishing season opened. Everyone waited for the run of sea trout to come up the river. Why? Because they were bigger and stronger and fought harder than landlocked trout, and because the flesh was pinker and tasted better too.

Donald and I only got to go fishing together once in a while, because we usually went with adults. We used long, bamboo poles with green cotton fishing line wrapped around the tip with a cork as a float, a small piece of lead as a weight, and a hook with a worm as bait. We dug our own worms in an unoccupied flower bed or garden and put them in a small soup can with some earth to keep them fresh. We usually only fished from the river bank because we didn't have a boat, and our parents wanted us to fish close to home. So we'd stand or sit on a piece of driftwood or a rock and watch for the cork to bob.

We never had much luck fishing trout because we

didn't have the patience. It just wasn't exciting enough. However, when the gaspereaux came into the river later in the spring, we also fished for them together using an open mouth trap that we made from chicken wire. This was more exciting for sure. These fish came up the river every year to spawn, travelled in schools and swam along the shore in shallow water. They usually swam against the current and chased each other in circles, paying no attention to us on the rocks or our homemade net open to the current. They were also easy to see because of the flash from their silver sides as they swam right into our makeshift trap. We had a short piece of rope attached to the top of the open end, so when we got a few in the trap, we'd pull the trap out of the water, haul it up on the rocks and take the fish out with our bare hands. We had to be careful because the underside of a gaspereaux is razor sharp.

When we had enough, we loaded our catch into the wire parcel carriers on the front of our bikes, took some home to our mothers and peddled the rest around the village, selling them for five cents each. This continued for the next few days until the fish moved on or the women of the village got tired of us, or both. Gaspereaux are notorious for having a lot of bones, making them difficult to eat, but they were tasty and fresh and a treat at that time of year. They are still fished commercially each year on the S.W. Margaree River in Cape Breton, packed in salt and shipped to the West Indies for human consumption.

At this same time of year and later lone harp seals would appear in the basin of the river between the two bridges also hunting for a feed of fish. Because they were known as a long time threat to trout stocks, an alarm was sounded. One of the many shotgun-toting trout fishermen would come out onto either bridge, and when the seal came up for air, they'd shoot it. Days later the carcass would wash up onto the river bank on a high tide and lie there until scavengers ate it or it washed away on another tide. One day Donald and I went to see a dead seal on the marsh near the railway bridge just below the school. It looked as big as a small cow, with a head almost the size of a horse's.

One spring when we were still very young, Donald and I were playing down by the river, and Donald was wearing his uncle's hip waders. There was no guard rail at that location. The tide was so high that it was lapping at the edge of the road. Donald reached for something, lost his balance and fell in. I couldn't reach him, so I screamed for help, and Ira Birt came running from the forge, which was close by. All we could see of Donald in the water was the red soles of his upturned rubber boots. Ira grabbed the boots, and luckily one stayed on, so he was able to pull Donald out, coughing and sputtering but okay. Of course, he was soaking wet and had to go home to change, but he came right back out none the worse for the experience.

Chapter 50

Slings and Arrows

I don't know where we got the idea, maybe from older boys, but in springtime, when we were ten or eleven years old, Donald and I would walk the woods between the village and Fanningbrook in search of the perfect 'Y' to make a sling shot or a bow and a collection of arrows. We both carried pocket knives and sometimes a small axe or hatchet. Our first sling shots came from alders at the back of Walsh's pond near home, but the wood in them wasn't very good, so they broke easily.

When we got back home from the woods, we peeled the bark off our find, cut them to the length we needed, and made them ready for the rubber bands that gave power to the slings. These we cut from one of the flat car inner tubes that were always lying around. Flat tires were almost a weekly occurrence in those days. We borrowed one of our mothers' scissors to cut the inner tube, and one of us would hold while the other cut. We always tried for straight pieces, not from the curve of the tube, which helped to make the stones fly straight. Besides, similar straight bands looked nicer. We cut extra in case one broke, all the same length and width, to allow for an even pull and a straight shot. Then, we'd pick four of the best, two for each of us, and fasten them to our slingshots with white cotton string from the grocery store. One of us would fold one end of a rubber band around an arm and stretch it tightly with thumb and fingers, while the other wrapped and tied the string to hold it in place. We'd repeat this until both our slingshots had two bands securely attached.

On the other ends of the bands we'd attach a small patch of soft leather to hold the stone to be shot. We usually salvaged the leather from the tongue of an old pair of men's leather shoes. Hopefully the owner wasn't still wearing them! With our pocket knives, we'd cut narrow slits in each end of the leather, suitable to attach the rubber bands. Again one of us held the folded end of the rubber band and stretched it, while the other tied the string as tightly as he could.

Next, we'd gather some small stones and go somewhere away from the buildings and windows for a trial run. Our target might be a fence post, a tin can or an empty beer bottle, and we'd practice until we were satisfied with our new weapons. If not, we'd go back and complete the necessary adjustments.

Occasionally, the target might be a stray cat or a bird, only with the intent to scare, rarely to injure or kill. On an extended trip into the woods we'd always take our sling shots and a supply of small stones from the roadside or the railway in case a squirrel, crow or rabbit might be deemed worthy of a shot.

The bows and arrows were more difficult to find in the woods, because they had to be a certain size and as straight as an arrow. Pardon the pun! The bow also had to be close to the same thickness at both ends, or it wouldn't pull straight. Again we'd peel the bark off, cut everything to the required length, and notch the ends of the bows so the heavy string wouldn't slip off. The arrows too had to be notched at the big end to fit the string. We sharpened the tips of the arrows at the small end so they would stick in the ground where they landed and make them easier to find.

All of this carving was done with our pocket knives. We didn't have the luxury of metal tips or feathers for our arrows, just the wooden shaft as best as we could craft it. Our target might be a piece of cardboard, but mostly we just shot the arrows into the air to see how far or how high they would go. It was all good fun, but like most children's games, the novelty eventually wore off, and we'd move on to something else.

Chapter 51

Crows' Feet

No, not those lines that appear around the outside edge of the human eye of aging adults, but the real thing.

We're talking real crows' feet, and for a time they were worth real money. Around 1947 or 1948, Ducks Unlimited or some like-minded organization offered to pay anyone who delivered a pair of crows feet to the local merchant, Adrian Feehan, the princely sum of twenty cents. "Why?" you might ask. Because on P.E.I. duck and goose hunting in the fall of the year was the only hunting for the average macho male over the age of sixteen with a hunting license and a shotgun. Crows were natural predators of ducks and geese and made an annual practice of raiding their nests, eating both the eggs and the young.

Donald and I knew that the intent of this bounty was to increase the chances of survival for more young geese and ducks, but we didn't really care. We both welcomed the chance to pick up a bit of loose change. By now we were both proficient in the use of sling shots and, after we got started, Donald was gifted with a brand new Daisy air rifle. Each spring, the marsh along the South side of the river in back of Walsh's pond was a favourite nesting area for both ducks and geese. Beyond the marsh, between the railroad tracks and the river, was a bush of scrub spruce and other trees that housed a colony of crows. Using road kill and stale raw meat or fish as bait, we managed to trap and kill several adult crows, borrowed their feet, and cashed them in.

Then we heard from a friend that Adrian was also paying for the feet of young crows. Now we were able to turn the tables on the crows by climbing the trees housing their nests when the adults were absent, being careful not to disturb the eggs. Because the nests were not far from home, we made regular visits to the crows' nests until the chicks were hatched. When they got big enough to recognize their feet, we drowned them, relieved them of their feet, and delivered them to Adrian. Neither Donald nor I remember the total haul from this enterprise, but the bounty money dried up after a couple of seasons so we moved on to other endeavours. For the record, our parents endorsed this activity, providing all of the captives were executed mercifully and not allowed to suffer.

Chapter 52

'Hookin Apples'

When we still lived on the farm, in good weather, it was common to see a man coming up the lane on foot or with a horse and wagon or in an old car. He was usually peddling something, selling merchandise door-to-door. A regular visitor in late spring or early summer was a man selling small fruit trees, because in those days, most farms and some homes in the village had an orchard, some new and some handed down from previous generations. We never bought any, because we already had an established orchard with apple, plum, and cherry trees, even a pear tree.

In summer, the first apple tree to bear edible fruit was what we called the Yellow Transparent or August White. These apples were sour at first but delicious when ripened, good for apple sauce and pies. The only knock against them was that their life span was short. If we didn't pick them in their prime, they soon fell to the ground, and before long they were bruised and rotten, suitable only for pig feed.

Barney and Me

In the village, we had no orchard, so when Donald and I were nine or ten years old, and the apples ripened on Mrs. Saul Clark's two Yellow Transparent trees behind her barn, the temptation was just too great for us to ignore. The trees were fully visible from our place, so one evening, after dark, we decided to go 'hookin', or stealing apples. We'd sneak across Reggie's small field, over the Peakes Road, and then across the railroad track. If a car came by, we'd lie down in the ditch until it passed, then crawl, commando-style, under or through the page wire fence.

We just picked the ones that were already on the ground, fumbling around in the dark, and we only took what we could eat that night. We never shook the trees, and we never told anyone else. It was a secret. We went back on other nights when the opportunity presented itself and there were apples to be had. We continued to return until the apples were all gone or no longer fit to eat.

As it turned out, we weren't the only ones stealing apples. Donald remembers another night when I wasn't with him and he went hookin apples with his cousin Lennie and others to a farm with an orchard at the Head of the River. Lennie, also known as 'Cheesie', climbed an apple tree in the dark to shake it, and a raccoon jumped on his back. That 'scared the livin daylights' out of Cheesie, and in the ensuing commotion he brushed the raccoon off his back, jumped down out of the tree, ran to the car with the rest of his buddies, and took off. The result was that there were very few hooked apples on that particular expedition, but lots of laughs, at Cheesie's expense.

Chapter 53

Tricycles and Bicycles

Around the age of eight, I was given a used tricycle of the larger variety. Daddy probably got it from someone in the city. Everything worked on it, but the paint was faded and it had signs of rust from the salt air climate. I had no concrete or pavement to drive it on just a mixture of dirt and grass in the driveways, so every trip was a struggle. After a rain, I had a selection of puddles out the back lane to drive through with my feet spread apart and off the pedals so as not to get wet. It was even more fun if Donald pushed me to go faster and then jumped on the back before we hit the puddle. We were not allowed to go out onto the main street which was paved, and we obeyed. At times I would go down Grampy's or Alden's driveway towards the river as fast as I could go with Donald standing on the back, screaming and laughing as we went. Occasionally we would wipe out with maybe a scrape or a bruise, but never a serious injury. The tricycle would be put away in the barn for the winter and be brought back out when the roads dried up in the spring.

Then one day a couple of years later, the tricycle was replaced by a bicycle that Daddy brought home from somewhere, a second-hand men's bicycle. It had a navy blue frame painted with a brush, a new maroon front wheel with a new tire and fender. The front fork was bent, so the back wheel didn't line up with the front, which made it even more difficult to balance or learn to ride. It also had a wire basket parcel carrier on front attached to the handle bar. It was the only bike on the block at that time, so it was a novelty, and it was better than walking, when we finally mastered the art of riding it. The bolt that held the seat in place was stripped, which allowed the seat to tip backwards whenever one of us managed to get on it. We corrected that by tying the front of the seat to the crossbar with an old hame strap from a horse's harness. That strap was still on that bike when it was finally retired.

The bike was too big for me at first, but with help from Donald and my older sisters and many tumbles and bruises, I finally managed a few solo wobbles out the back lane after they let me go. Their cooperation was followed by a chorus of "Let me try" or "No, it's my turn!" Then I would take my turn pushing, running, steadying and trying to increase the speed for each new wobbly rider. Eventually everyone that wanted to try got a chance, some with success. Donald, who was smaller than me, persisted day after day until he mastered the art of pedaling with one leg through the frame under the crossbar. He later got his own bike, so as we grew we could travel together, even on the paved Main Street.

One summer when I was ten or eleven, Donald wasn't with me, and I considered myself an accomplished bike rider, I came roaring down past the forge on my old blue bike and turned out onto the gravel River Road. I spotted a neighbour girl Pauline walking alone towards me coming from across the bridge. She was a bit older than me and in my eyes growing better looking every day, so I decided to impress her by driving straight at her, planning to swerve around her at the last minute and scare her. As I got close to her and swerved to my left, she dodged in the same direction. I ran into her with the front wheel and knocked her down. I fell off my bike, jumped up all embarrassed and tried to apologize. She got up, brushed herself off, gave me a disgusted look and asked, "What do you think you're doing?" We both parted and went our separate way, each with only a few scratches. She later told one of my older sisters, "Your dumb brother doesn't even know how to ride a bike."

By the time I became a teenager, my older sister Connie had acquired her teacher's license and was teaching in a one room school at Cherry Hill where our Mom and her brothers had all gone to school. She lived at home and walked or hitched a ride the nearly four miles to work most days. In bad weather she would stay at Uncle Harold's in Cherry Hill, across the fields from the school.

Barney and Me

The next spring, after a few pay cheques, she splurged and bought a brand new bike, a girl's bike, an Eatonia Glider with all the bells and whistles. It looked and rode like a Cadillac compared to my old clunker. She would let me ride it sparingly at first, when she wasn't using it. Then she became interested in boys with cars who would drive her to and from school. One of them, a young minister at our church, later married her. Gradually, I became the sole operator of this girl's bike and in spite of much jeering and teasing from other boys, I rode it proudly. Wherever I went on that bike, it was as fast as the bike would go. When I grew out of the bike, especially when I got my car driver's license, I handed it down to my younger sister, Muriel.

My Grade 5/6/7 class (me in jacket and tie on the left)
Taught by Mrs. Cummiskey

My grade 8/9/10 class (me in striped shirt in front)
Taught by principle McGuirk

Chapter 54

School Holidays

July and August were summer vacation away from school for Donald and me, except we started back to school in mid-August to allow for two weeks off in October to dig potatoes. The first holiday after we started back to school was Thanksgiving. To Donald and me, like other school children, Thanksgiving meant we had no school on Monday. It also promised at least one sumptuous meal on Sunday after church, with all available kinfolk coming to join us and leftovers for the first part of the next week. The meat for the main course might be roast beef or pork, chicken, duck or goose. No turkey, unless you were a farmer who grew them or could order one from someone that did. Dessert was a variety of pies, pumpkin being the most popular, also apple, cherry, lemon, raisin and more.

Although we didn't get a holiday from school, Halloween was one of the most memorable nights of the fall season. In The Block we did door-to-door visits, trick or treats, but what we collected in treats wouldn't fill a one pound paper bag. Apples were still a treat, were given out freely and received without fear of razor blades. Costumes were homemade and simple. There were no pillow cases full of loot being carried by children wearing expensive store-bought costumes.

A memorable Halloween for me was when my grandfather Coffin passed away two days before my tenth birthday. I was sad, but also disappointed that I couldn't go trick or treating with Donald and my other friends.

Halloween was also an opportunity for some older teenagers and young adults to play tricks on neighbours near and far. Wise citizens always made their visit to the outhouse before dark on October 31st, definitely before the bigger goblins came calling. Tipping over the outhouses of the village grouches was a popular sport on Halloween. The prime targets were those from whom the tricksters could get the most reaction, like hollering or swearing from a window or doorway or threatening a load of coarse salt in the ass from the muzzle of a shotgun.

Soaping windows or throwing rotten eggs at someone's house or car were minor pranks without major consequence. Removing gates from their usual place and hanging them on the cross arms of the nearest railway crossing sign or in a tall tree was also a prank for the older set. Dismantling a farm wagon and re-assembling it on the barn roof at night, so as to greet the farmer at day break, was for the strong and daring. Other mischievous acts included taking sleepy hens from their roost and perching them on the front seat of the family car. Anyone who has visited a hen house knows what lies on the floor under the roost. Another trick was harnessing cows with harness from the horse stable. The cruelest of all pranks was painting a large pig with lead based paint, which was the most common kind of paint used to paint steel bridges. At best it would make the pig sick, and at worst would kill the animal. This was not intentional, but it did happen.

While Donald and I were not big enough to help, one Halloween night we watched a group of adults, including women, pick up the body of an old car, minus engine and drive gear, carry it from behind the White Rose service station near the highway bridge out onto the street and set it down at the North end of the bridge to block it off. Then they hid in the shadows to see how the Mounties were going to get around it on their next patrol.

After Halloween, the next holiday from school was Armistice Day, November 11th, when we were encouraged to attend the 11:00 AM service in front of the War Memorial in the People's Cemetery at the south end of the village. Veterans in uniform, clergy, dignitaries, church choirs, old and young, some walking on their own, some needing assistance, all attended. If they could, they were there. Hardwood chairs from the church hall were provided for those who had difficulty standing for the hourlong service. A church pump organ was delivered earlier that morning by truck and a few strong men. My father, if he was not away working, was one of the organists who played for that annual event. After the service, the organ was loaded back onto the truck and returned to the church.

Next came Christmas and New Years with the whole week off from school, when we were free to sleep in, and I'd do only the most necessary chores to keep the home fires burning. Before Christmas, Donald and I would go to the woods, chop down a couple of trees and drag them home, hoping for our Moms' approval. We'd saw off the tree butt and attach it to a wooden stand. Then everyone would help to decorate the tree and hang our stockings for Christmas Eve.

We'd attend and maybe participate in Christmas concerts in the memorial hall and perhaps other schools, just nights before the big day. We'd also attend at least one church service. Donald and his family always went to Midnight Mass on Christmas Eve.

On Christmas afternoon, weather permitting, we'd visit friends and relatives and have more food and drink, compare gifts from Santa with our cousins, and maybe try out some new games or toys. We felt fortunate if we got one major gift like a new sleigh, a hockey stick or a pocket knife. Our stocking might have a mouth organ (harmonica), a new pair of socks, home knitted woolen mitts or stocking cap, an apple or orange or both. For days before, we might have been threatened by the adults to behave or we'd get a rotten turnip or a lump of coal

234

in our stocking, but that never really happened.

Valentine's Day didn't give us a day off but brought free time in school where we were provided paper and scissors to make valentines for our parents and friends. There were some pretty rough looking hearts cut out, but the intentions were good. The finished valentines had to be delivered by hand in the classroom for all to see us blush when we gave them. At home, the results of our labour were greeted with enthusiasm, no matter how rough the art work appeared.

Easter came with the promise of spring, longer days, more sunshine, melting snow, ditches full to overflowing with rushing water, high rubber boots and the shedding of at least one layer of winter clothes. Most of all it meant another full week's holiday from school and softer snow for snowball fights or building snowmen. To me it also meant two or three days at Uncle Harold's in the country with cousin Garth, who was one year younger, driving horses and hauling logs out of the woods on the snow drifts still remaining along the edges of the fields. I also played one-on-one street hockey with Garth between the side of the garage and the barn doors, until long after dark some evenings. We also went trout fishing through the ice at Warren's dam if the season was open. On stormy days, in the shed of the barn, Garth and I started to build wooden crates for next summer's strawberry season. Then on Saturday night, exhausted at the end of the three days, we would drop off to sleep lying on the dining room floor with blankets and pillows, listening to Foster Hewitt broadcasting the hockey game from Maple Leaf Gardens on a battery powered radio. Oh yes, don't forget how much I enjoyed all of aunt Alice's good cooking, like homemade bread, biscuits and cookies.

Finally, back to school for another couple of months until summer rolled around again.

Warren's Dam

Ice fishing

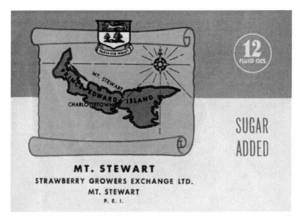

Label for strawberry jam canned in Mount Stewart

Chapter 55

Strawberries

For years before Donald and I were born, the strawberry was a king cash crop every month of July for farmers who knew how to grow them. The acreages of the average grower were relatively small, no more than two or three acres, and most growers kept a first, second and third year crop, in three separate plots. The first year strawberry plants were big and strong, and the berries were usually bigger than the next two years. The second year berries were a bit smaller than the first, but sometimes produced a comparable yield. The third year berries were smaller but sweeter, the choice of the ladies who made strawberry jam. In the fall, the third year strawberry plants were ploughed down, except for the best of them that were kept for replanting the next spring, and so the crop rotation went. In all situations, the berries were picked as they ripened and hauled to their destination on the evening of the same day.

While Daddy was still farming, he was one of the few farmers nearby who grew strawberries commercially.

He had less than an acre of berries. In the afternoon of a day's picking, he would take the back seat out of his 1928 Chevrolet, load the space with crates of berries, and pedal them around neighbouring communities where there were few other growers. He charged twenty cents a box. Sometimes my sisters and I would go with him. When door-to-door sales petered out, he dropped the unsold berries off at the cannery in the village.

In the loft of the cannery were long rows of tables with benches where mothers and children who were old enough hulled and culled strawberries in the evenings so the berries were ready for canning the next day. After we moved to the village, when Donald and I were seven or eight years of age, we both had the pleasure of sharing this task, if our mothers could persuade us to go with them. We usually sat still long enough to hull a few boxes, then found an excuse to goof off and do something more to our liking. The mothers were paid so much a box on whatever they and their kids had hulled. The moms reserved the right to keep all the money and give the kids their share for the midway at Old Home Week in the city in August.

Then one year the cannery closed and was replaced by a new building down by the river called the Strawberry Exchange. Late that summer, after the cannery closed, a shipment of canned berries that had gone bad and fermented was returned by the buyer. The cannery staff dumped them out the elevated back door onto the ground behind the building. Shortly after, Donald and I wandered over to the old cannery when nobody else was around. We discovered these rejected cans scattered among broken cardboard boxes, and we could see the cans were under such pressure that both ends were bulged out. As we each picked up one of these cans, Donald glanced at me and said, "hand grenades," and we both hurled them at the nearby concrete foundation of the building. They cracked open, hissing like snakes, while berries and jam sprayed all over the wall. This was great fun. We laughed and threw a few more cans, with the same result. Then the light went on, and we realized that if we got caught we'd have to clean up the mess. We dropped the last two cans and fled. We never heard a thing about it afterwards, and we didn't speak of it either, to anyone.

Prior to working at the Exchange, both Donald and I picked strawberries for different growers outside the village for four cents a box, the going rate. I hated picking strawberries. My last year in the field at my uncle Harolds, I graduated from picking berries to gathering boxes of berries behind other pickers. I used a carrier that held ten boxes. When it was filled, I carried it back to the headland and transferred the full boxes into crates that held fifteen boxes each. (I had helped my cousin Garth build some of these creates when I was on Easter vacation the previous spring.) I stacked the full crates on top of each other until they were seven or eight crates high. Then I started a new row, and another, until the picking was finished for the day. In the evening, I helped load them all onto a truck for shipment to the Exchange.

Chapter 56

The Exchange

The summer I was fifteen, I went to work at the Mount Stewart Strawberry Exchange down by the old wharf on our side of the river, barely a city block from home. In fact, it was built on the site of Grampy's old fox ranch. The Exchange replaced the old strawberry cannery, which was moved from its original location over next to the Exchange and used as a storage building. A strawberry season is three to four weeks long, and during peak periods the Exchange ran two shifts, one day shift and one evening shift. I worked in the berry fields most days and then worked the evening shift at the Exchange.

My job at the Exchange consisted of taking boxes of berries out of the crates that were stacked on both sides of my station on an elevated platform and feeding the berries to the new washing/hulling machine as fast as I could. The machine, which we called the 'budder', had a sloped deck of high speed rollers that carried the berries down to a conveyor belt, removing the hulls from most of them. Above the deck were nozzles that sprayed water down onto the berries, washing them, and also washing away the hulls. Once on the conveyor belt, the berries passed by six or seven women on each side of the belt, picking out the damaged, green or rotten berries, and pulling the hulls off berries that the machine had missed.

Donald worked at the far end of the conveyor belt where the berries dropped off the belt into a large tub. When a tub would get three parts full, Donald and another man pulled that tub aside and replaced it with an empty tub. They then added white sugar to the first tub, and mixed it into the berries as a preservative. Then they moved that tub over to the packing table, where a team of ladies scooped the berries into margarine-sized tubs, weighing and covering each tub, then packing them into cardboard boxes for shipment to the cold storage facility in the city.

The day shift at the Exchange was staffed by mostly local men and women, but management brought in a charter bus load of mothers and daughters from the Rustico area of north shore P.E.I. for the evening shift. I learned years later that this part of the Province is affectionately known as 'the Crik', which was slang for creek. Most of the ladies from Rustico spoke broken English, but were fluent in their mother tongue, Acadian French. The daughters were fluently bilingual. They were a cheerful, friendly, hard working group who had a sense of humour and seemed comfortable with the job.

Each evening, half way through our shift, we got a fifteen minute smoke break, and the adults and teenagers congregated separately outside in the dark where the lights shone from inside the Exchange. One cute teenage girl with red hair and freckles, starting to show her femininity, was bolder than the rest. She seemed to like me and took pleasure in teasing me more each evening. One evening, she came close to me, while we were standing in the shadows on flattened card board boxes, and whispered "Voulez-vous couche avec moi?" With my limited high school French I eagerly replied, "Oui, Oui, Oui." She laughed heartily and ran away from me saying, "But I did not say, 'ce soir'." That's as close as I got to her, and she never let me forget it. I think her name was Sophie. She was gone as soon as the strawberries were done, and I never saw her again. Here entered religion as a serious obstacle, as she and most of her community were Roman Catholic, and I was Protestant. Were it not the case, I might have borrowed Dad's car and tried to find her in her home community.

When I say that religion was a serious obstacle, I mean it. My grandmother Jay had a litany of 'real life' stories from our village and surrounding area about how good, clean living young people got tangled up with boys or girls from the wrong religion, married them, had children, and then had their adult lives become horror stories afterwards, living together, but going to different churches each Sunday morning, one with the children and the other alone.

Chapter 57

Ice Cream Festivals

When I was a boy, almost every little community on the Island had its own one-room school house that, in addition to being a school, was a gathering place for meetings, Christmas concerts, dances, and ice cream festivals. The latter was the highlight of the summer, usually near the end of the strawberry season, for adults and children alike. My favorite was at Cherry Hill school, where Mom and her brothers had attended. Donald attended other similar festivals, but I don't remember the two of us being at Cherry Hill together.

Preparations were made for days before. Someone loaned a stationary gasoline, water cooled engine, perhaps from the thrashing floor at home. Someone else borrowed an electric generator to be driven by a belt from the engine to light up the school and the yard outside, because there was no electrical service to that area. The festival started in late afternoon and went on into the night. There were games for children, like sack races, where we pulled burlap potato bags up to our waists, held onto them with both hands and hopped like rabbits, try-ing not to fall, which is what we usually did several times during the race, laughing with the cheering spectators. We'd get back up and try again to reach the finish line, bag and all. We also ran three legged races, where we chose partners, tied our right ankles to their left ankles with a piece of binder twine, put our arms around each other's shoulders, and raced against other teams, made up of boys and girls our own age. There were also other races where we would run flat out and try to win against other children our age.

Outside, the men had built a homemade rough board dance floor, usually a day or two before. It would be big enough to hold two or three square sets at one time, dancing to the live music of a fiddler and a guitar player, if one was available. The dances were later in the evening and mostly for adults, but older children were welcome. After all, we were a big part of the festival, and that was where a lot of us learned to dance.

There was also a bowling alley outside, built of rough lumber. It was perhaps thirty feet long and three feet wide with a backstop also made of boards to keep the balls close by. A V-shaped trough was built out of rough boards and elevated on stakes at the far end where the pins were set up, gradually sloping to the front end so that the balls could be returned to the bowlers. There were three well used bowling balls and one old set of five pins borrowed from the YMCA in the city. Older boys would be detailed to take turns as pin boys for the evening. I recall it was an honour to be chosen for that job when I was old enough and a bigger honor to pay my five cents to throw three balls at the pins. The balls felt like they weighed a ton, especially held in one hand. The bowling alley had its own string of lights, maybe four or five bulbs over top of the alley, supported on high poles at each end. Sometimes just when a bowler was about to throw the ball, the engine driving the generator would miss a stroke and the lights would dim momentarily, but it usually recovered in time for the bowler to continue.

Treats consisted of hot dogs, sandwiches and sweets, all kinds of homemade good things to eat, but above all there was homemade ice cream. Earlier in the day, ladies had mixed the ingredients at home and kept them cool on ice. Not all housewives had the equipment or the knowledge to make this wonderful stuff, but some would bring a freezer from home, if they had one. Others would donate blocks of ice from their ice houses and a chisel or ice pick to break pieces off the blocks, so they could be packed around the metal cylinder that contained the ingredients inside the barrel of the wooden ice cream maker.

The ice cream maker had a metal driveshaft and gears attached to the top of the barrel as well as the top of the cylinder. It also had a hand crank on one end that caused the cylinder to rotate in the ice. Inside the cylinder was a two-bladed wooden paddle that stirred the goodies as the cylinder turned. An adult usually started the churning, and once everything was deemed good to go, any and all adults and children strong enough to turn the crank were invited to take their turn. Smaller children were welcome to keep the inside of the barrel around the cylinder filled with small pieces of ice.

The process usually took from thirty-five to forty minutes to achieve the finished product. To children, that seemed like an eternity, even if they were helping. The ice cream was served in dishes or cones, if we had them, with strawberries or chocolate on top, no charge! What a glorious treat, to be relished by everyone and treasured in memory until the next summer. The following day, if the weather was fine, the whole structure had to be dismantled, the parts returned to their owners and stored in a safe place until festival time next summer. Unfortunately, with the advent of regional schools and the closure of one-room schools came the demise of the country ice cream festivals, but we still have the memories.

Chapter 58

Blueberries

To the eyes of two young boys, looking for a much anticipated break from work, it seemed that the strawberry season had just ended when the wild blueberries began to ripen. Armed with pots and pans and other empty containers of all sizes, Donald and I were dispatched, like many other neighbourhood children, to anywhere within walking distance where wild blueberries grew and where we might not get in trouble for trespassing. Some favourite spots were along the Georgetown railroad track and by the fence line of adjacent fields. If there was no fence, then we just kept picking into the field. We could count on the railroad property producing a bumper crop of berries every second year, because the section men burned the grass and bushes along the tracks every spring to keep the bushes from taking over and making the property unsightly. Blueberries don't like competition, and the annual burning allowed them to flourish.

Although commercial pickers may have beaten us to the punch at some spots, most times there were enough berries left for us. Adults who picked berries for money usually had hand-held pickers that resembled metal dust-pans with the handles inside and short knitting needles soldered to the leading edge, like so many tiny fingers. Their picking was likely full of green or rotten berries, leaves and other debris that had to be graded out of the finished product later. Our hand-picked berries had only a few undesirables among the good ones. Each day we delivered the fruits of our labour home to our mothers and, after assessment, we were allowed to take the sur-plus across the bridge and sell them to one of the buyers, Clark's or Affleck's, for between five and seven cents a pound, depending on how clean they were and how much they needed berries that particular day.

When we were older, we joined our friend Kevin in his father Jimmy's warehouse, or our friend Gerald, with his father John W., to help with grading the berries, separat-ing the good berries from the bad and other 'culch' that gathered on the conveyor belt after they passed through the blower. Basically, we were helping to get the berries ready for shipment to cold storage or directly to market. Neither Donald nor I can remember if we ever got paid for these short jobs, probably just happy to be helping our friends. Both of us enjoyed working with blueberries better than strawberries anyway.

Chapter 59

Forty-five Gallon Drums

As far back as I can remember, and long before that, there were always lanterns, lamps and kerosene oil to burn in them. Every household had a one gallon galvanized metal can that they would take to the general store and get filled when it became empty. It had a large metal screw cap on top that covered the hole through which the can could be filled, and a similar smaller screw cap on the spout to keep the can from leaking if it tipped over. The can also had a small wooden handle that hinged on the top for carrying and filling lanterns and lamps. Sometimes, if the small cap from the spout got lost, the merchant would stick a small potato or onion on the spout to keep it from leaking.

As oil burners in kitchen stoves replaced or supplemented coal and wood-burning fire boxes, there came a need to have larger oil containers outside the house. Here enters the forty-five gallon drum. It was a large round barrel, navy blue in color, with flat bottom and top, the latter with at least two holes in it called 'bungs'. One was for filling and emptying, and one was to allow air in while draining. These holes had caps that threaded into them to seal them for transport. The drums weighed between four and five hundred pounds when full and were usually filled with stove oil, furnace oil or diesel fuel. The most popular approach for homeowners to hold the drums was to build a wooden stand with a cradle on top that held the drum lying on its side. It had to be strong enough to support the weight and high enough to allow the oil to be gravity fed into the stove inside the house. A copper tube would be attached to one of the bungs, fed through the wall of the house behind the stove, and connected to the oil burner.

If delivery by oil truck equipped with a long hose was available, then that is how the drum was filled. If not, a full drum would be delivered on a flat bed truck and rolled off onto the ground. The empty drum would be taken away by the truck driver. It was usually up to the home owner to recruit some help to get the new one up onto the stand and into the proper position. All able bodied men, women, and older children would be invited to help roll it up a couple of strong planks to its resting place. Once the drum was started up the planks, we dared not let it slip, or it would roll back down, and we would have to start over again. There was always the danger of injury, because of the sheer size and weight of the full drum. So if it did get loose, someone would holler, "Look out, she's gonna go," and everyone would scatter, laughing and stumbling and perhaps cursing, but ultimately turning and coming right back to try again. This operation was always much more precarious in winter, due to the slippery surfaces and lack of traction.

A few years later came the oil fired heater that was equipped with its own detachable gravity fed tank of a gallon or two. Then the outside drum had to be refitted with a tap to fill the smaller tank.

Finally came the below the floor oil fired furnace, which was a God-send in winter. Some of these models are still in use today. These furnaces required a greater volume of oil, so the two hundred gallon oil barrel was created, and that spelled the end of the forty-five gallon drum for household use.

Chapter 60

Telephone Office

When Donald got old enough to be left alone on a weekend afternoon, he'd have to operate the switchboard in the telephone office, and sometimes I was there to help him. Basically, if he was left in charge, he was totally in charge. I never took or made a call. He wore the headset, and I just kept him company. The only problem was that we couldn't leave. We had to stay there until an adult returned and took over.

In the early days, when the switchboard was battery powered, the system was low voltage, just enough to ring the bell on incoming calls and send the outgoing ring when Donald turned the crank. When the switchboard was quiet, Donald, the prankster, would hold a plug for an outgoing call in his hand, pull the toggle switch back and turn the crank. He'd get a mild electric shock, according to him. I suspected it was mild to him due to his high tolerance for pain. He passed the plug to me and said, "Here, you try it," and when he turned the crank, I got a jolt. He did the same thing to Lennie, and Lennie dropped the plug. Each time, Donald would throw his head back and laugh, and we'd call him a nasty name or even curse at him, or Lennie might hit him on the shoulder, as he so often did when Donald would torment him. Donald just laughed at us some more.

Later, when the switchboard was changed to electric, it was 110 volts. That was a different story. It no longer had a battery but an electric ringer. Before I ever got to see it, Donald had already checked it out. This time when he offered the plug to me, I refused. He reluctantly demonstrated how he could still hold the plug and activate the ringer. When I looked closely, his fist was contracting around the plug. Wisely, he held it only for a few seconds then shut the ringer off. Afterwards, he claimed that while the ringer was on, there was no way he could open his fist, but he had no apparent ill effects. On another day, he tried the same thing with Lennie, and like me, Lennie refused. Otherwise Donald was all professional. When someone came in with a problem or called about something, he was the perfect, helpful little operator. He listened in only to check if people had finished talking, so he could disconnect the line.

During really quiet times, Donald and I would go across the hall into the parlour. Donald would pick up his guitar and play something, and I'd accompany him on the piano. I could chord on the piano because I was used to playing along with Daddy on the fiddle. We were a musical family. Making music of some form was a common occurrence most days in our house. When Donald and I got warmed up, laughing and singing, we made all kinds of noise, because nobody else was there. The time passed a lot quicker, and we had fun! When we tired of music, we'd play cards, or just go sit in the sun porch to watch the cars go by until someone else came home to take over the switchboard.

Chapter 61

Women Drivers

As an indicator that male chauvinism was still alive and well, Donald remembers that in the late 1940s there were only five women drivers in the whole village. As there was no driver testing program in place, all any adult had to do was get someone to teach them how to drive and then write a letter to the city requesting a driver's license.

One of those women drivers was our neighbour, Helen Walsh, who at first didn't have a car, but later bought a light grey 1947 Plymouth sedan in very good condition from a local merchant, Billy MacLeod. Another was Violet Affleck who drove her husband's car when he was at work. Some neighbours used to say that the engine in that car hardly ever had a chance to cool off. Barbara McAskill, drove a Model 'A' Ford and, as they say, especially to church on Sundays. The fourth woman was my Mom, Marion, who drove our family car, a 1933 Frontenac sedan, while Daddy was away working during the week. She had been taught to drive by her eldest brother Doug when he returned from the First World War and bought a car in the early 1920's. The last woman driver in the village was Shaud Sheppard, the doctor's wife.

Every year during the Music Festival in Charlottetown, these ladies and Rev. William Mercer were readily available when children of families without a car needed a ride to the city to compete in the festival. There were no school buses and no buses of any kind in our part of P.E.I. As the festival was on for a week, many trips were made back and forth to the city by these willing volunteers.

In summer, when Mom had the car home, she had to drive to Georgetown or Souris on Saturday evenings to pick Daddy up and bring him home. One Saturday afternoon, after considerable begging by Donald and me, she took us with her in the Frontenac to Souris to meet Daddy. I sat in the front seat with Mom, and Donald sat in the back. I pulled rank on him. We got along fine until passing through the community of Five Houses we met a runaway team of horses pulling an empty truck wagon. They were a terrifying sight coming full tilt towards us, ears back, harness flapping, the remnants of the load and the reins dragging on the road.

Mom's greatest fear was that the reins dragging behind the horses might get caught in a wheel and steer them over into our path. She slowed the car and pulled over almost into the ditch, just as the team blew by. Then the car engine stalled. Try as she might, Mom couldn't get it going again. Before long two nice young men in a logging truck came up behind us, stopped and offered to tow us in to Souris just a few miles away. Mom accepted, so they hooked a short chain from the truck onto the driver's end of the front bumper, and we started out. Early in the trip, the truck lurched ahead, there was a snapping sound, and the chain tightened. From then on, Mom had trouble steering the car. She blew the horn several times to get the truck driver's attention, but he didn't hear. Going downhill when the chain went slack, the steering was better, but there was always the fear that we would run into the back of the truck. The short chain didn't help Mom's situation. Each time the chain tightened going uphill, the steering problem came back. Mom hung onto the steering wheel with all her might and kept her foot over the brake. Finally, after what seemed like an eternity, we arrived at a garage in Souris.

As the men unhooked the chain from our car, they discovered that the front bumper had broken away from the frame at the end where the chain was attached. That caused the other end of the bumper to pivot and press against the front tire on the passenger side every time the tow chain tightened. Mom thanked the two men for the lift, and they went on their way.

The mechanic tied up the broken bumper with some wire, and Daddy got it welded later in Mount Stewart. When he examined the car engine, the mechanic discovered that the rotor button in the distributor cap had cracked, so the engine couldn't get any spark for ignition. He replaced the button, the car started, and Mom paid him. When the train came in, we drove to the station to pick Daddy up. Boy, did we have a story to tell him!

Chapter 62

Clark's Boatbuilding

Before the advent of steel hulled, steam driven ships in the late 1880s, Mount Stewart and the area South along the Hillsborough river towards the city was the home of several shipyards that turned out ocean-going wooden ships, complete with mast, sails and cargo in the hold. They were sold to the buyers as a package. The cargo was lumber, grain and other products from the forest and farms surrounding the village, and was hauled dockside by horses pulling dump carts or truck wagons.

The story is told that the driver of one of those carts was a young man from Fanningbrook who became my great grandfather Jay. As he drove through the village with a load on its way to the wharf, a beautiful young lady was sitting on the veranda of what later became Donald's home. My great grandfather was so enthralled that, on his return, he stopped the horse, jumped down from the cart, walked up to the young lady on the veranda, and boldly said, "I'm going to marry you," and he later did.

So much was the demand for grains in markets overseas that farmers with small farms were tempted to plant oats or barley in the same field year after year. This practice eventually exhausted certain nutrients in the soil, so that the farmers of my father's generation were obliged to replenish the PH balance with the only thing available, 'mussel mud'.

The mining of mussel mud was done in winter, from the frozen surface of a pond or inlet, using a giant fork that was supported by a huge wooden structure and powered by a single horse and capstain. The very heavy mud was then loaded by hand onto a horse drawn wood sleigh and hauled to a nearby railway siding. There the mud was manually shoveled onto a flatcar with side boards and shipped by rail to another siding, near the farmers who ordered it. The farmers then unloaded the mud from the flat car by hand into their horse drawn dump carts or wood sleighs, hauled it home to their farms, and spread it on their fields. If the railway placed a time limit on the flat car, some farmers were faced with dumping their loads onto the ground, near the siding and reloading most of it to take home the next day. My father told me that this had happened to him when he was younger. Talk about a labour intensive exercise!

Moving ahead to our time, there was only one boat builder in the village, Eddie Clark, who operated from a barn in his back yard. Eddie built wooden inshore fishing boats by himself, until his son Georgie joined him and learned the trade. A neighbour across the street, cousin Art, told me that in the late 1940s, Eddie sold a forty foot boat to a local fisherman for $800.00. The price did not include cabin or the engine, just the boat. Art estimated that Eddie probably built nine or ten such fishing boats in his lifetime. Donald and I both visited Eddie's boat shop at different times, and we were fascinated at seeing such a large boat under construction. Eddie was a kind, quiet and skillful man, who spoke softly and smoked a pipe. That made him distinguished-looking to us.

Georgie was three or four years older than Donald and me, so we didn't know him all that well. Donald remembers Georgie as a protector of younger boys our age, rather than a bully, of which there were a few where we grew up. Donald recalls being at a dance at the Memorial hall with his cousin Lennie one night when a fight broke out, which was not uncommon. Georgie was there, and he took Donald and Lennie across the street, where they could watch the fight but not get involved in it.

When Eddie retired, Georgie carried on the trade in a newer, larger facility, in the nearby village of Morell. He specialized in fiberglass boats, and when he got going his shop could turn one out every six weeks. These boats were longer, wider and heavier than the wooden boats, but less sea-worthy. Some owners even poured concrete into the keel in an attempt to lower the center of gravity and help stabilize the boat. Georgie's shop also added a fiberglass skin to existing wooden-hulled fishing boats.

Soon, Georgie became known to be very skillful at his craft, and there was a high demand for his boats, but he built too many, and they lasted too long, and the market for them dried up. Also, Georgie didn't wear any masks or respiratory protective equipment while working with molten fiberglass. He was also a heavy smoker of cigarettes. Eventually, he was stricken with throat cancer and died after a long battle against it. The consensus was that the cause of death was his constant exposure to fiberglass and tobacco products during his lifetime.

Chapter 63

Daddy's Sun Porch

In the early years in our home in the village, which had been built by out-of-work shipbuilders in the mid 1800s, we had a seasonal porch to cover our back door in winter. Daddy would put it up in the fall, take it down in spring and store it in the barn. Four or five years later, after World War Two, Daddy, once a farmer and carpenter, now a full time railroad trainman, decided to build a permanent porch. He called it a 'sun porch' because of the number of windows he put into it, and that's what the neighbours called theirs. It would fill the L-shaped corner where the kitchen joined the main house near the back door. Daddy attached the new porch so that the wooden shingles on the outside of the main house, remained visible inside the completed porch. He did most of the work himself in his spare time, with some help from Grampy and me. I was ten or eleven at the time.

To support the outside corner of the porch, Daddy dug a hole by hand at least three feet deep and placed a large flat rock in the bottom. On the rock he placed the end of a steel pipe which stuck out of the ground when the hole was filled in. He explained to me that the hole had to be deep enough to keep the frost from heaving the porch in the winter. He gathered lumber, new and used, and he bought used windows from a demolition project at the airport. Inside, at the end of the porch next to the main house, he added a combined storage closet and wood box, accessible by a narrow door. High in the closet he built shelves and drove nails into the house wall to hang winter jackets and work clothes. He shingled the roof with early style asphalt shingles that interlocked in a method called 'v-lock', and he fastened them with galvanized shingle nails. He shingled the porch walls below the windows with wooden shingles. I helped by handing them to him from the bundle one at a time.

One fine summer day when Donald was with me, Daddy asked us to go to the garage to get another bundle of wooden shingles from in front of the car, which was parked front-on in the garage. I owned a flat-bed wagon that Daddy had made from an old buggy axle with two wooden wheels, a wooden deck and two short wooden shafts to pull it. We decided to use the wagon to haul the forty some pound bundle of shingles out of the garage, rather than try to carry it. To access the bundle with the wagon, we just had to move the car. A year or two before, Daddy had built and installed two new wooden garage doors that hinged on the outside and came together in the middle. They were held shut by a large hook fastened to a removable vertical 2x4 secured in wooden pockets, top and bottom, inside the door frame. He had copied the doors from Grampy's garage doors and painted them red to match the other doors on our barn.

We entered the garage through the stable, unhooked and opened the doors, and braced sticks against them to keep the wind from blowing them shut. I felt like a big man when I could reach the hook without standing on my tip toes. I then opened the driver's door of the car, sat in behind the wheel, pushed in the clutch, shifted the gear into neutral, confident that I was big enough to reach the brake pedal if need be. Donald went to the front of the car prepared to help push it backwards. I stepped out onto the floor and pushed backwards on the door frame, while holding the steering wheel in my left hand. As the car started to move, I jumped in and closed the door, so it wouldn't catch in the wall or door post on the way out. I wanted to steer it to my left to a parking spot in front of the house, so it wouldn't block the back lane. As the rear wheels dropped off the door sill, the car gained speed. Too soon I cut the steering wheel to the left, and the tip of the front bumper caught the right hand door casing, pulling the casing and the door almost off the garage, leaving the door dangling by the lower hinge.

Daddy was still working at the back of the house, but he must have heard the commotion and came to investigate. He was not pleased! Not only was the garage door damaged, but the right front fender had a crimp in it above the wheel. The car was a 1939 Chevrolet sedan, dark blue, seven or eight years old, but in good shape. This was only the third car he ever had, and cars were very important to Daddy. With an air of disappointment and some disgust, he examined the combined damage, started the car, and backed it over to where I intended to park it. After all this, he probably carried the bundle of shingles to the back of the house himself. Work was resumed, the garage door was fixed, the car fender repaired and painted, and eventually the sun porch completed. Such was my first ever car accident, and sadly, not my last.

I now have four sons and six grandsons and can certainly empathize with Daddy on that day.

Our family with the Chevy that tore off the garage door

Barney with my cousins Carl, Arthur and Wayne

Chapter 64

Teen Dances

Most of us can remember those awkward, early teenage years, attending a social gathering at a school or house where there was music and older teens and adults were dancing. The stress level increased considerably when someone older and of the opposite sex came out of the crowd, grabbed us by the hand and dragged us out onto the floor. If we resisted and squirmed away and if the pursuer was not too persistent, we got away with it that time. Sooner or later though, we'd end up on the floor, willingly or not. The older we got the more the pressure to participate increased, especially if there was a girl present that we had a 'crush on' and couldn't muster the courage to cross the floor. In our day, this was solely up to the boy. The girl who made the first move was deemed not to be a lady.

Donald and I were no exception, we both had these experiences, perhaps not at the same time or place, but we talked about them together. Eventually, at about age fourteen or fifteen, we started attending summer dances at school houses in Fanningbrook, Head of Hillsborough, Cherry Hill and Pisquid East, all within ten miles of the village. We usually had to hitch a ride there with someone we knew. Opportunities improved considerably when Joyce's brother Gerald got his driver's license and borrowed his father's half ton truck. We'd plan the evening beforehand, spread the word, and cram as many as we could into the cab of Gerald's truck. The rest, usually boys, rode in the back. Legally, only three were allowed in the cab. As we made new friends at the dances, like Willard MacKenzie with his father's 1950 Ford half ton, and Reggie Peters with his own 1951 Ford coupe, things were really looking up. In most cases, the boys went to dances stag and took their chances that a girl their age would be willing to dance with them and perhaps permit them to take her home.

I got my driver's license the fall I turned sixteen, so the following summer, Donald and I were really rolling, so long as Dad gave me his car. One night Donald and I left home, picked Joyce up in Cherry Hill, drove to Fanningbrook, picked up Doreen, and went to the dance at her school. Most dances were square dances, with one or two round dances thrown in during the evening. The final dance of the night was usually a waltz. This was the last opportunity the guys had to ask that special gal if he could take her home.

Live music was usually provided by a couple from Pisquid West, Alvin and Thelma Burke, he on the fiddle and she on the guitar. If they were not available, another fiddler, Francis MacKinnon would play, accompanied by Alton Jay on the guitar. If there was a piano in the hall, the fiddler might also be accompanied by a piano player, usually a lady.

When we got older and bolder, we broadened our horizons and went dancing in late spring, summer and fall to the Saturday night dances in St. Peters, twenty some miles east of Mount Stewart. There we danced to the music of Don Messer and his Islanders. This was a really big deal, because Don Messer, the fiddler, was from the city. He played regularly on radio station CFCY and at concerts when invited. Although Don himself, the lead fiddler, didn't always play for the dances in St. Peters, his substitute 'Cec' MacEachern was no slouch on the fiddle, ably assisted by the rest of the orchestra, Waldo on piano, Duke on bass, Vic on drums, and Marg and Charlie singing duets.

People came from miles around to those dances, and it was there that I first laid eyes on Mary 'Bus' MacCallum. She lived right across the road from the dance hall. She was very pretty and had many suitors, but I managed to persuade her to have a dance with me most nights. Later that year she agreed to accompany me to my Grade XII prom at Prince of Wales College in Charlottetown.

Although dress for everyone was casual, the gals usually wore a dress or skirt and cotton blouse, or a sweater in cooler weather. The guys wore plaid cotton shirts with sleeves rolled up and shirt tail tucked in and the white cotton T-shirt showing out through the open neck. On the bottom we wore blue jeans as new as possible with the pant cuff rolled up one turn showing the inner side of the pant leg and white socks. Most of us wore leather-soled shoes to make the dancing easier, regardless of the floor surface.

When I was about fourteen, Daddy took me to Billy MacLeod's store to buy me a new pair of dress shoes. The last box on the shelf held a pair of black shoes with laces in the side. I really liked them, so I tried them on. The left one fit okay, but the right one seemed a bit big. I took them off, and we checked them. We found the left shoe was a size 10 and the right was 10 and a half. A brief discussion with Billy led to the conclusion that a previous customer must have bought a similar pair with different sizes and never noticed or brought them back. Because they were the last pair in the store and I needed new shoes, we agreed to take them. On the way home, Daddy suggested that before I wore them I should give them a good coat of polish to preserve the leather and keep them looking nice. I got out the shoe-shine kit and polished them up. They looked like 'a million dollars', and I thought I was the 'cat's meow' heading out to my next square dance. My right foot has been bigger ever since.

One memorable feature about the friends Donald and I travelled with during those very impressionable years was that none of us drank booze of any kind. There were plenty of bootleggers selling all kinds of alcohol to adults and teens, even moonshine. Some of us smoked cigarettes, because that was the macho thing to do, but none of us drank liquor. I've been forever grateful for that, because I believe whatever mischief we may have gotten into would have been much worse had we been drinking.

Some of the young men, a bit older than us, did drink, and a few were inclined to start trouble at dances. Although men from the same community tended to band together if a fight broke out, they could hardly be called a gang, but sometimes the loser of a fight at last week's dance would carry his grudge forward and bring along reinforcements to the next dance. Our friends only got involved in a fight if we had no other choice. Otherwise we steered clear and were given a wide berth. In spite of the possibility of fights at dances, none of the sponsors hired bouncers. At St. Peters, however, a Mountie, named 'Silver' from Souris Detachment would come into the hall when he was on duty and stand with his arms folded and his back to the wall just inside the door. He would scan the crowd, rarely speak to anyone and only stay a little while, but his mere presence and the possibility that he might return seemed to quell any notion of fighting at least for that night. I know he definitely had an influence on my decision to join the R.C.M.P. a few years later.

Chapter 65

Stirring Hormones

As we grew up, feeding off conversations from older men and boys, the topic of sex eventually led to our own erections. In our homes, Donald and I had both, on occasion, caught a glimpse of an older sister in various stages of undress. That aroused us slightly and gradually introduced us to the joys of manhood. From boyhood in the village, it was quite acceptable for us to pee outside, as long as we made an effort to find a secluded spot and not display our wares. As small boys, to add a little flourish to peeing, we might pinch the end of our foreskin and fill it with pee, then let it go, laugh, wipe our hands on our pants, and carry on. In winter, we'd try to write our initials in the snow. As we got older, during a stop to relieve ourselves in the daytime, we'd compare penis sizes, whose was the longest and whose was the biggest around. We'd laugh and tease each other, but never resorted to mutual touching or masturbation. For me, that was left to the privacy of my own bedroom.

I will never forget one warm spring evening, when

Barney and Me

I was twelve or thirteen. Donald wasn't there, but a neighbour girl, Mazie Davis, came to play outside with my younger sisters and some other girls. Mazie was a jolly, playful girl who was beginning to 'set all the bricks in the right places'. Strangely enough, I was invited by the girls to join in a game of tag, or hide and seek, one of those where you chase each other around the house. We took turns being 'it', and as darkness came, I remember chasing Mazie and, with her cooperation, easily catching her in a corner of our house near the back door. For a fleeting moment, with nobody else near us, she allowed me to hold her face to face and press her against the side of the house. I was taller than she was, and if we were not so shy, we could have kissed, but we didn't. I don't know if it was the thrill of the chase or what, but then and there, I had my first erection in close proximity to a girl. We parted and joined the others with questions like, "Where were you?" and "What were you doing?" coming from the others. Neither of us answered, and we never spoke of it afterwards. That summer her father was transferred to another town, and I never saw her again.

Later that same year, probably in winter, we were at a church Young People's meeting in the home of a shirt-tail cousin, Marsha Anderson. She was older and much more developed than the other young ladies present. We were playing musical chairs, where there is always one less chair than people dancing around them. One time around, Marsha was just ahead of me when the music

277

stopped, and she quickly sat in the empty chair, reached out and pulled me onto her lap. She began tickling me and the smell of her perfume and her touch caused me to have an instant erection. I blushed, pulled myself away from her and disappeared into the hall until things cooled down enough for me to rejoin the group. She knew what she had done and laughed heartily with a knowing glance when I came back into the room, still blushing. I probably told Donald about this later.

Once I was at my Uncle Harold's farm on a warm summer Sunday afternoon with my cousin and good friend, Garth. Our Uncle Charlie's family had just arrived home 'from away' earlier that weekend, and all the adults were in the house catching up on the latest news. I was fourteen and Garth thirteen, the same age as Donald. Charlie's two daughters, Leslie and Linda, were my age and starting to get 'bumps in all the right places'. For something to do, the four of us decided to walk back the quarter mile to Kimble's deserted old farm, to see if the Yellow Transparent apples were ripe yet.

Kimble was a cousin of Garth's father who had previously left the old homestead and moved in to Head of Hillsboro to live with Mom's Aunt Euphemia and her husband Calvin. Kimble was a middle-aged bachelor farmhand with a perpetual grin, a great sense of humour, and missing front teeth. At family gatherings he took great pleasure from sticking his head in amongst a bunch of teenagers, preferably girls, and asking one of them,"Didja get the notion yet?" and then watching closely for their reaction. They'd all giggle and laugh and act surprised, but they really weren't because they had already heard of Kimble's reputation from older brothers and sisters.

On the way back to the farm, Garth and I got fooling around with the girls, pushing and shoving and teasing each other. When we got to the old orchard, the apples were still green and not fit to eat, so we went exploring around what was left of the old property. The girls sat down on the ground near the cellar of the old house, and we joined them, all in a happy, teasing mood. There was some fine sand in a dry spot on the ground and the girls from the city started gathering it, picking it up and running it through their hands. They feigned at throwing some at us, but thought better of it. Then they started pouring the sand down the front of their V-neck T-shirts while laughing at us and watching for our reactions. Because they were bent over, we had full view of the tops of their budding breasts. Then they'd shake the sand out the bottom of their shirts, so we'd see their bare bellies. Garth and I just watched, partially shocked and partially aroused, and too stupid to accept the invitation, real or imaginary. We walked together back to the farm and never mentioned it again to the girls, but Garth and I discussed it once or twice with combined feelings of guilt and perhaps some of masculine inadequacy.

Barney and Me

Every summer, Mom's family and some of her brothers' families gathered on Sunday afternoons, weather permitting, for a picnic on the land above the beach at Savage Harbour, on the Gulf of St. Lawrence, about six miles from the village. Most of the adults would sit and chat near the sand dunes or on the beach while the kids would go swimming. Boys in swimming trunks and girls from age four to sixteen in bathing suits would play in the breakers not far from shore. Very few of us could swim, and there were always warnings about the dreaded undertow, which is when a large wave recedes and takes the feet out from under you, just as another hits your upper body on its way to the shore.

The water was usually cold, and the macho boys and some girls would run out into it and fall down. Most girls including Leslie and Linda would gingerly enter, splashing water gently on their arms and upper legs. The boys would run after them and splash them just to torment them. When we all got wet, we'd continue to splash and push each other into the waves, and two boys might grab a girl and throw her into a wave, just to hear her scream. The boys might also be hoping for a feel of soft flesh in the bargain. The girls would threaten us, squeal and scream, but kept coming back for more until we all had enough.

We'd go ashore and grab a towel, and some of us walked along the beach and talked while we dried off. Then we'd come back to old linen table cloths, one for each family, spread out on the ground all in a row above the beach, held down by rocks on each corner, so the wind wouldn't upset our picnic lunches. The children would dive into a spot around their family table cloth and ravenously consume their allotted sandwiches, sweets and drinks, and head out to play some more, this time not in the water. I will never forget, and neither will my cousins, our ferocious appetites and the sheer joy and pleasure of those Sunday afternoons, now so long ago.

I also remember how Donald and I used to visit Marsha in the egg grading station in the back of Clark's Butcher Shop. There was a separate side entrance to that part of the building, and we'd come and go as we pleased. Marsha worked in a dark room to examine each egg for flaws by holding it up to an encased yellow light. It was a boring job for her, and she seemed to welcome our company. We got a kick out of being alone with her, an older woman, in the dark, while she worked. When she found a rotten egg, or one with a clot in it, she would lean aside to show it to us. This proximity to her and the smell of her perfume gave us both a 'fuzzy' feeling, and we liked it.

One afternoon, in early summer, when the both of us were hanging around outside the shop, an older boy from up country driving his father's new car dropped by to see Marsha. We recognized him and knew that he had a reputation of freely sharing his charm with other young ladies in the area. After some friendly teasing and banter between them, he persuaded her to go for a ride in the car with him. She reluctantly accepted, and they were gone, not for long, but long enough, we surmised, for a little afternoon delight, although we had no idea exactly what that was. We waited, and before long they came back. He dropped her off, did a u-turn, stirred up some dust, and was gone. Marsha got out of the car all smiles, walked past us and went back to work without a word. Oh, how we envied that boy from the country with his dad's new car and his apparent success with the ladies! We teased her about it later, asking her what they really did while they were away, and she just laughed at us.

Chapter 66

Winter Vacation Adventures

At age eighteen, I left home February [1], 1956 to join the R.C.M.P. boot camp in Regina, Saskatchewan, a train trip of almost five days. Donald and others organized a small farewell party at our house the night before I left.

The next year, in March 1957, I returned home on my first two week annual leave. Donald was still home and attending a mechanics course at the Vocational School in Charlottetown. We picked right up where we left off, and we spent as much time as we could together with our girlfriends – Joyce, who is now Donald's wife of fifty-three years, and Doreen, who is sadly no longer with us. Dad still had his 1955 Plymouth and made it available to me anytime he didn't need it.

My second night home, cousin Carl came over to visit, driving my horse Dell in the box sleigh. As the evening passed, he persuaded me to come over to his place for a couple of days, so I went. As we drove along through the fields on a beautiful moonlit night, we were talking, and I was driving but not paying attention to where Dell was going. Without warning, the right runner of the sleigh ran up on a snow drift, and before we knew it the sleigh was on its side and we were both dumped out into the snow with our belongings, laughing our heads off. Dell stopped, turned her head and just looked at us. We righted the sleigh, put the parcels back in it, and went on our way to Carl's home.

Two other events of that vacation stand out in my mind, both involving Donald and Dad's car. One was a weekday morning after Donald and I had been out on dates the night before. As I dropped him off at home, I promised him that I'd drive him to the city the next morning. During the night we had freezing rain, and the following day as we started out we noticed patches of black ice on the highway. There was no sign of the sand truck, so I drove cautiously and got along fine until we reached the bottom of Wright's hill leading into the city. There was one car on the hill ahead of us, just creeping along. Half way up the hill, I gradually eased out around him, and as I got past him, the rear end of our car switched right, and I lost control. The car went straight into the left ditch and came to rest in deep soft snow. We couldn't get the doors open, so we crawled out the windows. The car I had just passed went on its way, probably with the driver chuckling to himself.

In no time the sand truck came along, with two guys that Donald knew, because he had worked with them the previous summer. After they laughed heartily and got their 'jabs' in at Donald and me, the 'good driver', they took a long tow chain out of the truck, hooked it onto the back of their truck and gave the other end to Donald to hook onto a rear spring of Dad's car. As the driver backed the truck towards the car, the helper spread sand behind the rear wheels for better traction. I got back in behind the wheel of Dad's car, and when Donald gave the 'Go' signal, that car popped out of the snow like a cork from a champagne bottle. We checked it over and found not a scratch. We thanked the guys, swore them to secrecy, and we went on our way.

A few nights later, Donald and I were in Dad's car and picked Joyce up at her home in Cherry Hill, three miles East of the village. We drove to the city, picked Doreen up at her uncle's place, and went to a movie. It was already starting to snow. When we came out of the theatre two hours later, it was the makings of a really bad winter storm. No restaurant or parking with the girls that night! We dropped Doreen off at her uncle's and headed home at about 10:30 P.M.

When we got outside the city, visibility was poor, and the wind was blowing hard from the North East and forming drifts. There were no snow ploughs out and very little traffic. At times we were the only car on the road, and when we did meet another car, we could barely see the headlights until it was almost on top of us. We drove past the entrance to the village and continued on to Joyce's home. The last mile and a half was a sheltered dirt road with at least eight inches of deep snow. At times we could only just keep going forward. Dad's car had a V-eight engine, standard transmission and good snow tires, and I used 2nd gear most of the way.

When we made it as far as the Tannery crossroads, Donald offered to walk Joyce the last quarter mile. That gave me time to turn the car around, by working it back and forth in the intersection. I didn't have to wait long for Donald, and was overjoyed when I saw his flashlight coming out of the blizzard. When he got into the car a gust of snow followed him. He said it was blowing and drifting so hard, there was no sign of his own tracks on the way back to the car. We made our way out to the main highway without incident and were within half a mile from the village when we met a series of hard drifts with bare pavement in between. Because the wind was blowing from the North across a clear field to our right, the drifts were higher on the right side of the highway than the left. I tried to keep the car's momentum up as big hunks of snow flew up over the engine hood, and I stayed to the left as far as I dared.

Without warning, the right front wheel hooked into a big drift and climbed up onto it. At the same time, the back end of the car swung left, jamming the left end of the rear bumper into the pavement. When the car stopped, we got out into the blizzard and surveyed the situation. We knew we couldn't leave the car there or the snow plough or another vehicle might run into it.

Besides, I didn't care to face my father in the morning if we didn't at least try to get it home. There was no such thing as a cell phone, and there was no tow truck to call anyway. We decided if we dug the snow out from under the right front wheel, we might get it partly down to the roadway, thereby freeing up the left rear bumper. In winter, Dad always carried a snow shovel in the trunk, so we got it out and took turns, one digging cautiously beside and under the car, while the other one held the flashlight.

At first the front of the car was up so high that we could kneel on the paved surface and our heads would just touch the frame behind the right front wheel. As we worked, our faces became crusted with drifting snow, and the snow we had earlier moved away from beside the car was already drifting in behind us. But with Donald leading the way with his ever present sense of humour, we laughed and joked to keep our spirits up. Mindful of the danger, we watched and listened for any downward movement of the car. Finally, it settled slightly and that encouraged us to keep digging. Gradually, the front wheel made its way down almost to the road and the rear bumper came clear of the pavement. We shoveled out behind all four wheels to ensure traction.

I got in and started the engine and backed out of that drift and kept going until I found a bare strip of pavement between two drifts. Donald climbed in with the shovel, and I gunned it into the storm. We arrived home safely in our front yard shortly before midnight, two very tired but happy young men. We had not seen another vehicle from the time we passed the village to take Joyce home.

The storm continued through the night but was over the next morning. We heard later that after we got out of the drift, another car got caught in the same area, and all that could be seen of it the next day was the roof top.

My winter vacation over, I said good bye to Doreen, Donald and Joyce and my family, and I went back to work in Nova Scotia with lots of fond memories.

My girlfriend Doreen with Barney going to the college prom

Sayings of the Day

Hush your tongue.
Bite your lip.
You and your bright ideas.
Well, look at you.
He/she haven't enough sense to come in outta the rain.
Crazy as a bag o hammers.
You go ahead and break the road.
He/She's drunk as a skunk.
He/She's loaded for bear.
He/She's lookin for a puck in the mouth.
He/She's blinkin like a toad under a harra (harrow).
He/She had a blank stare like a pig pissin.
It's black as tar.
It's white as snow.
It's hot as Hell.
It's cold as ice.
He/She's mad as a wet hen/hatter.
It's dry as a bone.
The wind was blowin like the mill tails of Hell.

Barney and Me

It's clear as a bell.
He/She's sharp as a tack.
He/She's hungry as a bear.
It's full to the scuppers.
It's loaded to the gunwals.
That separates the wheat from the chaff.
He/She looked like an unmade bed.
Many hands make light work.
Too many cooks spoil the broth.
That changes the water on the beans.
He/She's got the world by the ass with a downhill pull.
He/She's a goin concern.
I'm chilled to the bone.
He/She had about as much chance as a snowball in Hell.
Don't count your chickens before they're hatched.
He/She's sure got his/her nose outta joint.
It's goin like a bat outta Hell.
He/She's quiet as a mouse.
It's rainin cats and dogs.
So on and so forth.
Whatever suits.
It's not hittin on all fours.
Much obliged.
He/She got off on the wrong foot.
Just enough to take the chill off it.
Who died and left you boss?
They just made it by the skin of their teeth.
They're as scarce as hen's teeth.

Barney and Me

Don't be so foolish.
It's as smooth as silk.
Are you talkin or is that just yer ears flappin?
She/He looked a little bleary-eyed.
They were just out galavantin around.
She/He couldn't hit a bull in the arse with a boxcar.
Put that in yer pipe and smoke it.
Now, don't get carried away.
Monkey see, monkey do.
Yes, once in a blue moon.
He/She's three sheets to the wind.
She/He fell off the wagon.
She/He's back on the wagon.
She/He quit for lent.
She/He's squealin like a stuck pig.
If the shoe fits, wear it.
The shoe is on the other foot now.
She/He'd talk the leg off an iron pot.
He/She's poor as a church mouse.
He/She's dry as a chip.
She/He sure has the gift of the gab.
Git outta here before I grab ya by the scruff o the neck.
That takes the cake.
He/She's fat as a seal.
She/He fought like a cornered rat.
He/She had a face like a can of crushed worms.
It was like a bolt from the blue.
It's purrin like a kitten.

Barney and Me

It's shiny as a new penny.
Are you gonna break the ice?
Cross my heart and hope to die.
What's for ya won't go by ya.
I'm feelin kinda gaunt.
He/She's tryin to make a dollar outta fifteen cents.
You can't make a silk purse outta a sow's ear.
If you go ahead with that, there'll be Hell to pay.
You can't change the spots on a leopard.
She/He ain't worth a plugged nickel.
He/She's comin apart at the seams.
Go soak yer head.
Speak of the devil.
Sounds kinda fishy to me.
Keep yer shirt on.
I'm of a mind to give her/him a piece of my mind.
He/She's stickin out like a sore thumb.
She/He just didn't stroke his/her feathers right.
It's clean as a whistle.
He/She's deaf as a post.
He/She's slow as cold molasses.
He/She's stubborn as a mule.
It's like a hot knife through butter.
That'll separate the men from the boys.
I've talked about this til I'm blue in the face.
I'm sick, sore and tired of your shenanigans.
I'm fed up tryin to learn you to do things right.
Boy, did he/she ever read her/him the riot act.

Barney and Me

Now don't get all bent outta shape.
You'd be a good one to send for the devil.
The devil wasn't ready for him yet.
It's flat as a pancake/piss on a plate.
She/He's more to be pitied than scorned.
He/She's runnin ahead of the storm.
He/She's puttin up a good front.
He/She's a wolf in sheep's clothing.
May as well get hung for a sheep as a lamb.
He/She can really get under yer skin.
She/He can really get yer goat.
He/She's not too tightly wrapped.
He/She's wound up a bit too tight.
They're both tarred by the same brush.
She/He's a regular pain in the neck.
I'm sick as a dog.
He/She's busier than a one armed paper hanger.
There she/he was, hummin an hawin.
She/He drives a King's County pelter.
Not a star in her/his crown.
Look what the cat dragged in.
I could eat the North end of a skunk goin South.
They sure gave us a wide berth.
We're none the worse for the wear.
They were kickin up their heels.
You may well try to stop the tide with a pitch fork.
He/She just let the cat outta the bag.
She/He's just splittin hairs.

Barney and Me

It's straight as a bulrush.
Now that's a fly in the ointment.
She/He had a case of the flyin axe handles.
Don't get your bowels in an uproar.
She/He went by me like a bat outta Hell.
She/He's a few pickles short of a barrel.
Don't strain yer gizzard.
That's just cutting off yer nose to spite yer face.
No sense cryin over spilt milk.
Don't go putting the cart before the horse.
It's not worth a hill o beans.
Yer not particular about the company you keep.
She/He was so mad she/he was frothin at the mouth.
That engine wouldn't pull the hat off yer head.
I felt like I'd been pulled through a keyhole.
That sure came in handy.
He/She was jumpin around like a flea on a hot shovel.
That's like the pot callin the kettle black.
She/He looked like a dying calf in a snow storm.
All you can expect from a pig is a grunt.
Quit dilly-dallyin and get to work.
Outta the fryin pan and into the fire.
I'll be ready in two shakes of a lamb's tail.
Wouldn't that just rot yer socks?

About the Author

Allison Roland Jay was born in the family farm house in Fanningbrook, P.E.I. At age six, his family moved from the farm to the village of Mount Stewart nearby, where he met his friend Donald "Barney" Ross. At age eighteen, he joined the R.C.M.P. and served twenty-five years in Nova Scotia and Ontario. He worked the next fifteen years in Occupational Health and Safety with the Transportation Safety Association of Ontario. he is now retired and living with his wife Margaret in Rockwood, Ontario.

AL - 856-0441